MILITIAS

Armed and Dangerous

Kathlyn Gay

—Issues in Focus—

Enslow Publishers, Inc.

44 Fadem Road	PO Box 38
Box 699	Aldershot
Springfield, NJ 07081	Hants GU12 6BP
USA	UK

Library of Congress Cataloging-in-Publication Data

Gay, Kathlyn.
    Militias : armed and dangerous / Kathlyn Gay.
       p. cm. — (Issues in focus)
    Includes bibliographical references and index.
    Summary: Traces the development of the citizen militia movement from its
origins in colonial America through its modern involvement with racist and
neo-Nazi activities.
    ISBN 0-89490-902-9
    1. Militia movements—United States—Juvenile literature. 2. Right-wing
extremists—United States—Juvenile literature. 3. Government, Resistance to—
United States—Juvenile literature. [1. Militia movements. 2. Government,
Resistance to.] I. Title. II. Series: Issues in focus (Hillside, N.J.)
HN90.R3G275 1997
322.4'2—dc21   97-12528
                                             CIP
                                             AC

Printed in the United States of America

10 9 8 7 6 5 4 3 2 1

Illustration Credits: Southern Poverty Law Center, pp. 10, 66, 85; Bruce
Giffin, pp. 45, 60, 70; Author's private collection, p. 21; © Corel
Corporation, pp. 12, 14, 29, 33, 49, 51, 56, 78.

Cover Illustration: © Corel Corporation

Contents

1

Militant and Armed

In July 1996 twelve members of an Arizona group known as the Viper Militia were charged with conspiring to bomb local buildings housing offices of the Federal Bureau of Investigation (FBI); the Bureau of Alcohol, Tobacco and Firearms (ATF); and the Secret Service. The arrests of the Vipers followed a seven-month investigation by federal officials and an undercover agent who infiltrated the group. According to a *Newsweek* report, the infiltrator was a state game warden who posed as Scott Wells, a neo-Nazi (a member of a hate group against Jews and nonwhites). The secret agent "was accepted by the group—but not before he had sworn to kill, if necessary."[1]

During a court hearing to determine whether or not the Vipers should be jailed while awaiting trial, prosecutors showed a video that the group had produced in late 1995. On the tape members fire weapons and illegally detonate bombs in an isolated area in the Tonto National

Forest, approximately sixty miles northeast of Phoenix. Another video that members owned shows how to make bombs that cause buildings to collapse, and several local buildings were pinpointed—possibly as targets. Prosecutors claimed this was proof that the militia planned to create civil strife and obstruct the government of the United States.

Several months after arresting the Vipers, federal prosecutors revised the indictments against members of the group, dropping the accusations of conspiring against the federal government. However, other charges were filed, including the illegal "possession of destructive devices and unregistered machine guns," according to a report in the *Arizona Republic*.[2] While six of the group were released on bail, all of the Vipers face trial on various charges.

Revelations about the Viper Militia are among many other stories about militia groups that have surfaced since the mid-1990s. Before that time the majority of Americans were generally unaware of militias. In fact, few even knew how to define a militia.

A legitimate militia is a "citizen army," but it is not part of the regular army. Rather, as the United States Supreme Court ruled in 1886 (*Presser* v. *Illinois*), "all citizens capable of bearing arms constitute the reserve militia of the United States"; it is comprised of those eligible for the military who may be called to serve in a time of emergency.

The militias that are the focus of this book, however, are armed paramilitary groups—private armies. A paramilitary group is organized like a military unit, but it is not part of the military or of law enforcement.

Right-Wing Militants

Groups of "armed right-wing militants, most calling themselves 'militias,' are cropping up across America," the Anti-Defamation League (ADL) of B'nai B'rith, a civil rights group, reported in 1994.[3] Right-wing groups have been defined in numerous ways, but in simplified terms they are generally antigovernment or want as little government control as possible. Yet they believe in authoritarian rule that they themselves establish.

For the most part right-wing militants live by rigid religious beliefs and traditional family structures. Far-right extremists usually oppose—often violently—a pluralistic way of life, that is, a society with people from many different language backgrounds, religions, and lifestyles. They also advocate the overthrow of what they see as a corrupt government.

At the other end of the spectrum, radical left-wing groups may also be antigovernment and militant, but usually they oppose a government that does not establish programs and policies to benefit the total society. Militant radicals on the left, such as some antiwar demonstrators during the Vietnam War, have been as violent as extremists on the right.

Today's militant right-wing groups "have no centralized structure," but they share common attitudes and beliefs. They are universally opposed to gun-control laws, and they are "laying the groundwork for massive resistance to the federal government and its law enforcement agencies," the ADL reports. These extremists believe the federal government is "planning warfare against the citizenry. . . . The answer, say these extremists, is ultimately, necessarily, paramilitary resistance. An armed and aroused citizenry [in their view] must be mobilized and ready for a call to war."[4]

Those who believe they should prepare themselves for a civil war are predominately white. But a few black groups have formed militias, such as the Detroit (Michigan) Constitutional Militia and the Ohio Unorganized Militia. The Ohio group was cofounded by James "J. J." Johnson, who appeared before a 1995 Senate Judiciary subcommittee investigating militias. (In late 1996, J. J. was confused with James M. Johnson of Cleveland, who was arrested for his role in a plot by the West Virginia Mountaineer Militia to blow up a federal building in West Virginia.)

In testimony before the Senate committee, J. J. explained why his group exists: "People are tired of being terrorized by law enforcement. If a war is waged, these groups [militias] plan on winning. . . . If a police officer kicks down my door with no warrant, what am I supposed to do?" he asked, calling militias "the civil rights movement of the 1990s. We're not baby killers; we're baby boomers."[5]

Many militia members, including Johnson, declare they are patriots similar to the colonists who armed themselves to fight for independence from the British during the American Revolutionary War. However, the Patriots of today are part of a movement that has spread across the United States. They are attacking United

States institutions and resisting laws that they say interfere with their constitutional rights as they have interpreted the United States Constitution.

The Patriot Movement

There is no certain count of the number of Americans who call themselves Patriots, and estimates range from tens of thousands to millions. At the far-right end of the Patriot movement are white supremacist groups—those who think whites of northern European ancestry are superior to people of color, Jews, and others. Included also in the far right are white Christian Patriots who believe they are fighting satanic forces in the federal government and live only by "God's law." They hope to destroy the existing government and set up their own republic.

However, the Patriot movement "is not easily defined," notes a special report from the Militia Task Force of the Southern Poverty Law Center's (SPLC) Klanwatch Project in Montgomery, Alabama. The SPLC files lawsuits on behalf of those who are victims of attacks by white supremacists. Klanwatch was set up in 1979 to monitor Ku Klux Klan (KKK) terror tactics against non-whites and to provide help for victims. In 1994, because of the increased terrorism of armed militia groups, Klanwatch launched its Militia Task Force to track developments of the Patriot movement and its armed wing, the militias.

In 1996 the Militia Task Force, echoing the ADL, reported that the unrelated groups and individuals in the Patriot movement "have found a common cause in their

9

deep distrust of goverment and their eagerness to fight back." Patriots also share a conviction that federal and state officials are conspiring to disarm ordinary Americans in preparation for a "one world order," a government that controls the entire world.

Patriots base their one world government ideas on a myth about a Jewish conspiracy. That myth has been passed on for centuries and is based on a manuscript titled *The Protocols of the Learned Elders of Zion.* The manuscript stemmed from an essay written by members

"PATRIOT" ACTIVITY IN AMERICA

Number of "Patriot" groups in each state:
5 and under
6–10
11–20
21–30
over 30
state with groups engaged in paramilitary training
state with antimilitia and/or antiparamilitary training laws

Although it is impossible to determine the exact number of Americans who have allied themselves with the Patriot movement, estimates range from tens of thousands to millions of members.

of the Russian secret police in the 1890s. It is actually a forgery of an earlier publication—a satire on the French dictator Napoleon III. In *The Protocols,* the authors falsely claimed that a Jewish council planned to destroy Christianity and control the world.

"Calls for armed militias first surfaced in mid to late 1993, and they emerged from the militant fringe of the Patriot movement that began a slow but steady growth starting with the Gulf War and President George Bush's slogan calling for a New World Order," notes Chip Berlet. Berlet is an analyst at Political Research Associates in Cambridge, Massachusetts, and coauthor of several books about extremist groups. In an article posted on the Internet, Berlet and Matthew Lyons note:

> The fear that the United States was losing its sovereignty through international entanglements to groups such as the United Nations was a mainstay of reactionary organizations such as the John Birch Society begun in the late 1950s. The Birchers warned that Global One World Government was around the corner and for . . . decades the Society has pointed to a conspiracy of elites they call "The Insiders" [who] control the world through influential policy groups such as the Trilateral Commission and the Council on Foreign Relations.[6]

Economic and Social Factors

In some cases economic and social factors draw people to the Patriot movement. Some Americans feel "disaffected from and alienated by a government that seems indifferent, if not hostile, to their interests," explained

Many militia members believe that there is a conspiracy to create a "one world order," in which one government rules the world. Members fear that the United States is already losing sovereignty through its involvement with international organizations such as the United Nations.

investigative reporter Daniel Junas in an article for the spring 1995 issue of *Covert Action Quarterly*.[7] United States industries have relocated to other countries where wages are low, resulting in job losses, declining wages, and forced moves for many Americans. These displacements caused by the global economy create some legitimate gripes about one world trends. As Chip Berlet puts it:

> These are people who . . . had good industrial economy jobs. They've seen those jobs vanish. They're in the farm belt, the ranching fields, the rust belt.

They know that no matter what a bureaucrat in Washington will say about how there's been an economic recovery, they're putting meatloaf on the table Sunday night instead of a pot roast. . . . They're angry, and they have every right to be angry. Then weave into that the fact that a lot of these people are being asked, I think justifiably so, to give up privilege and power. These are essentially people who were challenged by the social liberation movements of the 1960s to share the pie. So you have people who are unhappy having to share power with people of color, with women, to look at the demands of the ecology movement, the gay and lesbian rights movement. All of these issues are in their face now. Look at it this way: It would be a lot easier to accept giving up privilege and power in a full-employment economy.[8]

Paul de Armond, research director for Public Good, an education project to uphold democratic values, has a somewhat different view about what prompts the increase in those who join the armed wing of the Patriot movement. In his opinion, "there is no militia movement" as such, but instead he calls it an antidemocratic thrust, "a tactic" throughout the nation to intimidate "by publicly promoting armed violence."

De Armond contends that an antidemocratic movement is the result of the union of white supremacists and the Christian Right (or Religious Right)—people who want a theocratic government, or rule by God, not a government of democratically elected officials. "These two extremist factions have found a way to 'mainstream' their message by forming an alliance with the radical right wing of the political spectrum," de Armond writes. The

13

Economic hardships caused by a global economy have increased the appeal of the Patriot movement for many Americans. Many farmers and ranchers have become disillusioned with the federal government, which has been slow to react to economic problems in the heartland.

groups gain power by suppressing the opposition of "responsible" conservatives, by attacking "abortion providers, environmentalists, immigrants and government employees," and by recruiting converts from "alienated white voters who feel cast aside from the national economy. . . . These tactics have made bigotry, prejudice and fear the predominant issues on the national political scene."[9]

Arming for Violence

Within the antidemocratic movement—or, as most call it, the militia movement—are those who follow Christian

14

Identity beliefs, an openly racist and anti-Semitic ideology that developed in Great Britain during the nineteenth century. In brief, Christian Identity teaches that Aryans—whites of northern European ancestry— are the chosen people described in the Bible. They say that the promises made to the nation of Israel (Jews) were meant for the British and the Americans. They call themselves "true Israelites" and claim that America is their promised land. They also believe that people of color are subhuman and that Jews are descendants of Satan.

Using a number of different names for their groups, Christian Identity believers promote paramilitary activities and armed militias. Their mission is to destroy people who are not "true Israelites." One early leader, the late William Potter Gale, a retired Army colonel who founded an Identity church in Mariposa, California, preached in a taped message broadcast in early 1983:

> Yes, we're gonna cleanse our land. We're gonna do it with a sword. And we're gonna do it with violence. "Oh," they say, "Reverend Gale, you're teaching violence." You're damn right I'm teaching violence! God said you're gonna do it that way, and it's about time somebody is telling you to get violent, whitey.[10]

In spite of the hate speech and numerous publications promoting violence distributed throughout the United States by Gale and other Identity leaders, their activities were not widely known during the 1980s. But as Identity followers and others who subscribe to similar beliefs formed armed militias in the 1990s, their illegal actions and calls for violence gained some attention.

By 1995 numerous militia members were convicted of such crimes as teaching people how to illegally avoid paying taxes and conspiring to kill federal agents and police. Conspirators have been found with hoards of weapons, materials to make bombs, and deadly poisons. In one instance, "four members of the Minnesota Patriots Council . . . were convicted in federal court for conspiracy to use ricin, a deadly toxin, to kill federal agents and law enforcement officers. The four would-be assassins had enough ricin to kill 1,400 people," according to the Militia Task Force.[11]

As in the past, many of today's militant militias believe they have the right to attack those representing authority and to commit terrorist acts. Yet "if every individual has a right to assault lawmen, there can be no government at all," notes investigative reporter and newspaper columnist Jack Anderson. "If everyone who turns up in the minority in some democratic decision-making process thinks he or she can overwhelm the majority with a spray of gunfire, society falls apart and nobody has any legal rights."[12]

That is precisely what a growing number of Americans fear. At the same time many citizens are unwilling to part with their guns and believe they have a long-standing right based on the United States Constitution to keep and bear arms.

2

Militia History and the "Right to Bear Arms"

Militias have been organized ever since ancient times and were part of European fighting forces until the 1700s and 1800s. In colonial America, militias were organized long before the war for independence. During the American Revolution colonies formed militias to be prepared to fight with the Continental Army against the British, if necessary.

Colonial laws required white able-bodied men to serve in militias, but not all colonies strictly enforced militia laws. Although men volunteered for the militia, many found ways to "avoid militia service by paying a fine or by getting an exemption," as militia researcher Sheldon Sheps of Toronto, Canada, and militia historian Mark Pitcavage of Ohio State University point out in their World Wide Web (WWW) postings about militia history.

On the Militia Watchdog home page maintained by Pitcavage, the two authors use the term "new militia" to distinguish between unauthorized groups that have formed in recent years and the National Guard and state defense forces established by federal and state laws. The extensive and well-documented information is presented, they say, as a means to provide "an accurate description of the history and law of the American militia. It is an antidote to the politically motivated butchery of history and misinterpretation of law by the new militia," writes Sheldon Sheps.[1]

Organized and Unorganized Militias

Contrary to the common belief that colonial militias were an unorganized mass of armed citizens, they were structured in pyramid fashion, like military units, with companies, regiments, and brigades under the command of a civil authority. Laws and charters of each colony determined how the militias were governed. Each colony's militia was organized so that local authorities or leaders could call up the militia to defend the colony. In Massachusetts, for example, the revolutionary government "directed all company officers to prepare one-third of their command to respond instantly to calls. Thus were created the Minute Man units, copied then by other colonies/states."[2]

Before and after the United States Constitution was adopted in 1787, intense debates centered on how militias—meaning the militias of the states—should function. The Constitution declares that the president is the "Commander in Chief of the Army and Navy of the United States, and of the Militia of the several States, when called into the actual Service of the United States."

18

But the United States Congress has the power to call "forth the Militia to execute the Laws of the Union, suppress Insurrections and repel Invasions; To provide for organizing, arming, and disciplining the Militia, and for governing such Part of them as may be employed in the Service of the United States." The states were given the authority to train and appoint officers for the militia.

In 1903 the militia was organized as the National Guard, independent of the regular army. Then the National Defense Act of 1916 mandated that the United States Army consist of the regular army, the reserves, and the National Guard, which later became a reserve unit of the army. Today there is also an Air National Guard. These units are considered organized militias of the states, United States territories, Puerto Rico, and the District of Columbia, and they are partly or wholly armed and equipped at the expense of the federal government. By law, states and territories may also have their own defense forces or militias that are regulated by state law. Oregon, for example, has a state defense force that is organized like the Oregon National Guard and works closely with that unit. Many states, however, have inactive forces that may be activated by the governor if needed.

Federal laws dealing with the militia refer to the organized militia or the National Guard. But Title 10, Section 311 of the United States Consolidated Statutes (USCS) refers to the "unorganized militia, which consists of the members of the militia who are not members of the National Guard or the Naval Militia." This section is often used by armed militias (new militias) to claim that they are actually part of state militias, and according to some arguments, should be organized and armed by the federal government and/or trained by the states.

However, Congress would have to repeal current laws and pass new legislation in order to organize the new militia. Court cases have determined that states generally are not responsible for training unorganized militia. In fact, new militia groups are not even militia in a legal sense unless they meet "the requirements of the United States Constitution, [and] federal and state law[s]," according to historian Pitcavage. Even if a group calls itself a militia that does not make it one, Pitcavage points out, because states create militia units under their own laws and federal statutes. A governor of a state is usually not authorized "to accept self-organized groups into a state militia structure."[3]

Legal experts generally agree that neither state nor federal laws authorize or protect the new militia movement. "Members of the new militia have no privileges, rights, duties, or immunities for their action over and above those of other members of society. The only way they can obtain privileges, rights, duties, or immunities would be by laws passed by either the federal or state government," explains Sheps in a WWW posting about the new militia. Yet, he adds, being unprotected does not mean that new militias are forbidden. "When these groups do things that don't break any laws, then there is nothing to stop them from doing them. When they do break the laws, there is nothing to protect them."[4] Nevertheless, members of so-called unorganized militias believe they are protected not only by federal laws but

Statement of Support for the Guard and Reserve

We recognize the National Guard and Reserve as essential to the strength of our nation and the maintenance of world peace. They require and deserve the interest and support of the American business community, as well as every segment of our society.

In the highest American tradition, these Guard and Reserve forces are manned by civilians. Their voluntary service takes them from their homes, their families and their occupations. On weekends, and at other times, they train to prepare themselves to answer their country's call to active service in the United States armed forces.

If these volunteer forces are to continue to serve our nation, a broader public understanding is required of the total force concept of national security — and the essential role of the Guard and Reserve within it.

The Guard and Reserve need the patriotic cooperation of American employers in facilitating the participation of their eligible employees in Guard and Reserve programs, without impediment or penalty.

We therefore join members of the American business community in agreement that:

1. Our employees' job and career opportunities will not be limited or reduced because of their service in the Guard or Reserve;

2. Our employees will be granted leaves of absence for military training in the Guard or Reserve without sacrifice of vacation time; and

3. This agreement and the resultant policies will be made known throughout the organization and announced in publications and through other existing means of communication.

Secretary of Defense

Chairman
National Committee for Employer Support
of the Guard and Reserve

Title:_____

Employer

_____ , 19____

Unlike unauthorized and armed militias, legitimate National Guard and Reserve units are an integral part of U.S. defense forces. During the early 1970s, a national committee was formed to encourage businesses across the nation to support the Guard and Reserve. A business that agreed to such support received this certificate to post in a public place.

also by the Second Amendment to the United States Constitution.

Second Amendment Arguments

The Second Amendment declares, in part: "A well-regulated Militia, being necessary to the security of a free State, the right of the people to keep and bear Arms, shall not be infringed." Over the years, some have argued that this militia statement applies to each state and its right to arm its militia—in other words, it is a collective right.

Others have contended that the term "the people" refers to individual citizens who are guaranteed the right to privately own firearms. This amendment has often been cited to justify the positions of those who oppose gun-control laws and by those who form armed paramilitary groups today. To right-wing extremists, the Second Amendment is an important guarantee of individual freedom. They argue that the amendment allows citizens to organize and arm themselves as a defense against a tyrannical government.

Controversy over whether the Second Amendment bestows a collective right for a National Guard or a personal right for each citizen to bear arms will probably continue far into the future. But the United States Supreme Court and state supreme courts have determined in several cases during the 1900s that states can control the use of guns and restrict gun ownership.

For example, in a frequently described case, the United States Supreme Court in *United States* v. *Miller* ruled in 1939 that Jack Miller violated a federal law banning the transport of sawed-off shotguns, silencers, and fully automatic weapons across state lines. Although Miller claimed the Second Amendment gave him the right to carry a sawed-off shotgun, the High Court ruled that his weapon had no "reasonable relationship to the preservation or efficiency of a well-regulated militia."[5]

In a Connecticut case, the state legislature passed a law banning sixty-seven types of assault weapons, and in 1995 the Connecticut Supreme Court upheld the ban as constitutional. Other state supreme courts—in Ohio and Colorado, for example—have also upheld bans on assault weapons.[6]

Still, some historians and analysts of the Constitution contend that the exact meaning of the Second Amendment and the issues it raises have not really been determined by High Court decisions. In the view of some legal scholars, "the amendment was meant to make citizens equal partners with government in ensuring individual and community safety," Aaron Epstein reports in a 1995 feature article on the topic for the *Philadelphia Inquirer.* He notes that law professor William Van Alstyne of Duke University, a respected scholar and teacher of constitutional law, "concludes that the Second Amendment developed out of a fear of a national standing army. It was intended . . . to protect the right of ordinary citizens who made up state militias."

However, this right, like other rights, is not absolute and does not prohibit some regulations on firearms. The amendment, for example, does not allow a person to carry a firearm into a school and "it doesn't mean private armies can be organized under the protection of the Second Amendment," as Van Alstyne states.[7]

Kenneth Stern of the American Jewish Committee, an expert on hate groups, emphasizes that Americans have means other than armed militias to guard against tyranny:

> The Constitution set out many ways to reform government, even to remake it entirely: Elections. Petitions. The free press. Impeachment. Constitutional amendments. No government provides for the right of groups of armed, disgruntled citizens to revolt by blowing up and gunning down government officials. That is called sedition, assassination, and treason, and is punishable by law.[8]

The Long History of Armed Militias

Even though private armies are unlawful, paramilitary groups have been on the American scene in one form or another for decades. During the 1930s, for example, one of the most dangerous was the Christian Front headed by Father Charles E. Coughlin, who believed that Christian civilization would be taken over by Jewish-supported communism. In a weekly radio program, Coughlin urged his listeners to "arm, train, and organize a Christian Front against the Red Front [communism]." He planned a paramilitary operation that was expected to grow to some 5 million troops, although the total number never came close to that.

Units did organize in many major eastern and midwestern cities, however, and they attacked Jews and Jewish-owned businesses. Recruits received weapons training "under the guise of sporting or rifle clubs," according to Philip Jenkins, professor of history and religious studies at Pennsylvania State University. Much of their ammunition came from army bases where military officers were sympathetic to the Christian Front cause.[9]

This was only one of numerous extremist organizations that flourished into the 1940s. The groups were motivated by events and conditions similar to those that prompt people to organize militias today, such as gun control and a changing economy. In Professor Jenkins's words:

> In the mid-1930s Congress passed the first federal gun-control law, banning the private possession of automatic weapons and machine guns. This aroused nothing like the furor over recent restrictions on assault rifles, but then as now such federal controls were depicted as an attempt to disarm the American people so they could be tyrannized—and then as now one response was military-style training and organization.[10]

Today's armed militias are motivated by still other factors. They justify their training and violent actions on radical ideologies such as the Christian Identity beliefs previously described. Another philosophy known as Posse Comitatus is closely associated with Identity churches, and it also guides militant militias.

3

Posse Comitatus

Posse Comitatus is a Latin term for "power of the county." Posse advocates believe they have the right to organize local governments with the local sheriff as the top elected governmental figure. The sheriff, they contend, should not be controlled by state or federal laws.

Henry L. Beach, who was once a member of a pro-Nazi group in the United States during the 1930s, organized armed Posse activists in Portland, Oregon, in 1969 and is one of the founders of the Posse movement.[1]

The late Identity preacher William Potter Gale, however, was the major leader in spreading Posse ideology. Gale not only set himself up as minister of a racist and anti-Semitic church in California, but he also conducted paramilitary training sessions from the 1960s to the mid-1980s. In 1987 he and four associates were convicted of plotting to kill Internal Revenue Service (IRS) agents and a federal judge, and interfering with the administration of income tax laws. They were sentenced to federal prison in January 1988. Four months later Gale died.[2]

Posse members are adamantly opposed to the IRS and the federal income tax, which they believe is unconstitutional. Why? Because the tax was established by the Sixteenth Amendment, which they say was not properly ratified. Thus they refuse to pay income tax as well as other taxes to support federal and state governments that they do not recognize.

One infamous Posse follower and tax resister was Gordon Kahl, a decorated World War II hero, who has often been described as a martyr of the Posse movement and Patriot causes. During the mid-1970s, Kahl joined the Posse in Texas and publicly announced on television that he would not pay taxes. He urged others to follow his lead, which soon led to his arrest. Kahl was convicted of tax evasion and sent to federal prison for five years, but he was released on probation after serving a year. Provisions of the probation required that Kahl stay away from the Posse and pay his federal income taxes.

In 1980 Kahl, his wife Joan, and their three children returned to a South Dakota ranch inherited from Kahl's parents. He was soon in trouble with the law again for not complying with requirements of his probation: he refused to file federal income tax returns. The IRS placed a lien on the Kahl ranch, a legal action to take property for money owed. Kahl still refused to give in to authorities and became a parole violator, insisting that it was time to "engage in a struggle to the death between the people of the Kingdom of God and the Kingdom of Satan."[3]

In February 1983 police set up a roadblock in North Dakota to stop Kahl and his son who was riding with him. In the confrontation, Kahl's son was shot and injured, two United States marshals were killed, and two others were wounded. After that Kahl became a fugitive, finding refuge with supporters throughout the Midwest, and then at an Arkansas home in the Ozark mountains. In June 1983 Arkansas police tracked Kahl to his hide-out, and a gun battle followed, igniting a fire that burned down the house. Kahl was killed, and at his funeral, was praised as a patriot. Ever since then some militants have considered him a hero, disregarding the fact that he was a lawbreaker who shot federal officials to death.

"Sovereign Citizens"

Posse Comitatus believers and others who share their views, such as Christian Patriots, claim to be "sovereign citizens." They contend that their natural and God-given rights exempt them from any legally established federal or state authority. Even a farm or building can be declared "sovereign" and beyond state or federal jurisdiction. As "sovereign citizens," they set up common-law courts and citizen juries that they say have the force of law, even though these courts are not valid in the United States legal structure. Since 1994 common-law courts have been set up in more than thirty states, and armed militia members work with these courts, attempting to enforce their decisions.[4]

Advocates also claim that common law covers only

Militant right-wing groups justify their plans for paramilitary resistance to the federal government and law enforcement agencies because members believe that the government is planning warfare against U.S. citizens.

white citizens, or "organic sovereigns" as they are sometimes known. According to Posse interpretation, only the United States Constitution and the first ten amendments are valid, thus so-called "Fourteenth Amendment citizens"—blacks and others protected by that Amendment—do not have the same inalienable rights guaranteed by the Constitution.

Reporter Michael Janofsky noted in a *New York Times* article that common-law courts

. . . . base their authority on highly selective interpretations of English common law, Bible passages, United States case law and the Constitution.

When they think that they have been wronged, they appoint themselves as judges, issue indictments and arrest warrants, and try cases, even though defendants generally ignore their trials and any judgment the court may decree. But the nuisance the courts pose are real, as are the personal threats and millions of dollars lost in their frauds.[5]

One major nuisance is a "paper attack." For example, when Posse members are investigated or arrested, they file liens against federal and state officials and those who speak out against common-law advocates. Although a legitimate lien allows a creditor, or person who lends money, to take property in payment for a debt, Posse claims are bogus. Nevertheless, they can cause a great deal of frustration, sometimes damaging a person's credit, or ability to borrow money and repay what is owed over a period of time.

Some Posse adherents have committed armed robbery and issued bad checks and counterfeit money orders totalling in the millions to support their cause. They use phony checks to pay off loans or they refuse to pay debts, which they say they do not owe, deliberately swindling corporations and public agencies. They insist loans are based on agreements that are not legally binding.

Township of Tigerton Dells

One Posse group involved in such frauds during the 1980s was located at a compound on the property of farmer Donald Minniecheske near Tigerton, Wisconsin. The Posse group established its own Township of Tigerton Dells. Members set up trailer homes, built underground shelters, conducted armed military training, and made no secret of their plan to rebel against the federal government. They also preached anti-Semitism and racist views in a pseudo-church called the Life Science Church of Tigerton Dells.

However, in 1985 the Posse's militant leaders—including Minniecheske and his son—were arrested and imprisoned on a variety of charges, including theft. Because of violations of zoning ordinances, county officials also removed trailer homes, sheds, and vehicles on the farmland. Ten years later a county judge ordered a raid on the property and law officials burned remaining buildings. The land was seized in payment for back taxes totaling $138,000, and the property was eventually sold to Shawano County to be used for a park.

Although it appeared the Posse Comitatus was out of business in Shawano County, officials say the group is still active under a new name, Family Farm Preservation (FFP). In March 1995 one of the FFP members, Thomas Stockheimer, was sentenced to sixteen years in prison for assaulting two police officers. He received the maximum sentence due to his previous convictions, among them battery and practicing law without a license. He was also indicted for fraud. Stockheimer and three other men distributed $65 million worth of forged money orders with instructions to recipients to use the phony documents to pay off mortgages and other loans. Like other common-law advocates, he believes it is unconstitutional for banks to issue loans. He falsely claims that the United States Constitution forbids using any currency except gold or silver coins to repay a debt.[6]

31

"Freemen"

Another group based on common-law ideas came to public attention in 1996. Known as the Montana Freemen, the group was involved in a tense standoff with the FBI. After eighty-one days in a compound called Justus Township near Jordan, Montana, sixteen Freemen surrendered to federal agents, ending what was a potentially explosive situation.

Several years before this standoff, the Freemen had set up their own government with their own common-law courts, laws, and monetary system. Like other common-law groups, Freemen accept Posse ideology and believe they are "sovereign citizens."

In 1994 the Freemen began stockpiling weapons, food, and other items on a 960-acre wheat and sheep ranch owned by Ralph Clark and his family. By the time the FBI surrounded their compound on March 25, 1996, others who called themselves Freemen, including women and children, had joined the group, living in several buildings. They refused to leave land that the Clarks had lost to bank foreclosures; the ranch had been sold at a sheriff's auction to recoup more than $37,000 Clark owed on a mortgage against the property.

However, during the standoff an FBI undercover agent lured two of the leaders, LeRoy Schweitzer and Daniel Peterson, away from the compound buildings, arresting them for conspiracy to impede government function and to prevent a United States district judge, a court clerk, and a county sheriff from carrying out their official duties. In addition, the men were charged with threats to kidnap and murder the judge, and faced

Many right-wing militia members stockpile weapons, ammunition, camouflage clothing, and bomb-making supplies.

indictments on fraud and other charges. Finally, in June 1996, all in the Freemen compound surrendered.

More Violence Executed and Planned

A few months after the Freemen surrender, still another dangerous group came to light. In early October 1996 Charles Barbee, Robert Berry, and Jay Merrell were arrested and charged with bombings and robberies in Washington State. The men are from Sandpoint, Idaho, an area where other antigovernment and militia groups make their homes.

Barbee, Berry, and Merrell claim to be members of the Phineas Priesthood, a white supremacist group

33

associated with the Identity church. The group is named for a biblical figure, Phineas, who killed a couple because they were involved in an intertribal marriage. Phineas Priests interpret this incident and others described in the Old Testament of the Bible as justification for their use of violence against "race-mixers" and efforts to establish an all-white republic.

In an attempt to carry out their mission, the Phineas Priests robbed a Spokane Valley, Washington, bank twice, on April 1 and July 12, 1996. Messages that contained biblical passages and were signed with the priesthood symbol were left at the crime scene. The Phineas Priests also are charged with bombing a bank, a Planned Parenthood clinic, and the office of the (Spokane) *Spokesmen-Review*, which had published articles against armed militias and supremacist groups. When federal agents searched the homes of the arrested men, they found "a large cache of weapons, ammunition, bomb-making supplies, camouflage clothing and flak jackets," the *Seattle Times* reported.[7]

Seven members of another armed group, the West Virginia Mountaineer Militia, were also arrested in October 1996. Although no connection has been made at this writing between the Mountaineers and the Priests, the two groups are organized around similar pro-gun and antigovernment ideas; they are preparing for armed conflict with the federal government. The Mountaineer Militia is led by Floyd Raymond Looker, who insists that the group is not antigovernment. Instead, he calls the members of his militia patriots and strong supporters of the Constitution.

Nevertheless, the group was "charged with attempting to collect and transport explosive materials with the ultimate aim of destroying the $200 million fingerprint facility in Clarksburg, W. Va.," according to the *Washington Post.* "Among those arrested was a member of the Clarksburg Fire Department, who federal authorities said provided photographs of the center's blueprints that were passed on to an undercover agent." Militia members thought the agent "was associated with an international terrorist group."[8]

Obviously groups such as the Freemen, Phineas Priests, and the Mountaineer Militia are not uncommon. In all areas of the United States small paramilitary groups organize, train, and plan terrorist acts. Also they are getting involved in political campaigns, hoping to advance their agenda. One part of their political activism, and a catalyst for the new militias, is to continually blame federal law enforcement agents for several tragic events that have occurred over the past decade.

4

Catalysts for the "New Militias"

Several highly publicized events during the 1980s and 1990s have convinced numerous militia members and white supremacists in the United States that their government is out to get them and that leaderless resistance is necessary. The Kahl shootout with law enforcement officials in the 1980s is one example. However, other tragic episodes during the 1990s have had even more impact.

The Ruby Ridge Incident

One early incident to galvanize the new militia centered on Ruby Ridge, Idaho, about thirty miles from the Canadian border. That is where Randy Weaver and his family had settled in the 1980s. Weaver was a former Green Beret and a white separatist—that is, he believed in living apart from nonwhites. He, his wife Vicki, and their children made their home in a crude log cabin on Ruby Ridge, a rocky outcrop where there was no electricity or telephone. They were linked with the Aryan Nations, a compound of neo-Nazis at Hayden Lake, Idaho, whose members revere Adolf Hitler.

Although the Weavers posed no threat to anyone, Randy Weaver was under federal surveillance. In 1990 he sold two sawed-off shotguns (illegal arms) to an undercover ATF agent, and afterward federal agents tried to use this to pressure Weaver into becoming an informant. They wanted him to report on Aryan Nations' activities, according to a published letter that Vicki Weaver wrote in 1990. Addressing the "Aryan Nations and all our brethren of the Anglo Saxon Race," she explained in her letter that two ATF agents had threatened Randy Weaver "with federal firearms charges and prison time and the confiscation of our truck."[1]

Weaver was arrested in January 1991 and claimed he was set up by law enforcement agents. He was released on his own recognizance, and with his family went to his mountain cabin, where he vowed to stay until his death unless authorities admitted that the charges against him were false. He refused to appear in court for a February trial on federal weapons charges.

Throughout the year federal agents monitored the Weavers' place and prepared to arrest Weaver again in August 1992. As law enforcement officials tried to get close to the cabin, one of them shot the Weavers' dog, precipitating a gunfight that killed Weaver's fourteen-year-old son Sammy, and William Degan, a deputy United States marshal. After the shooting, more than one hundred federal, state, and county law enforcement officials surrounded the Weaver cabin. The FBI also sent its military-style Hostage Rescue Team to the site with orders to shoot on sight.

The next day Randy Weaver unexpectedly left the cabin with his teenage daughter Sara and family friend Kevin Harris. Weaver was shot in the arm by an FBI sniper. When Vicki Weaver shouted at them to take cover inside, the FBI sharpshooter then fired into the cabin. According to a news report, "The bullet shot through the curtained window, blasted through Vicki Weaver's face, severing her carotid artery, and then hit Harris, tearing a lung and lodging in his chest."[2]

Harris was taken from the mountain and flown in a helicopter to a nearby hospital. Weaver, with his three children, eventually surrendered after an eleven-day siege. Both Harris and Weaver were charged with killing Degan, but a jury acquitted them. Later, Weaver won a wrongful death suit against the United States Justice Department, which resulted in a settlement of $3 million.

During 1994 a special Justice Department task force investigated the Ruby Ridge siege. The task force concluded that numerous mistakes had been made and that the shoot-on-sight orders were unconstitutional and unnecessarily dangerous. In the fall of 1995 a United States Senate subcommittee investigating terrorism in the United States found evidence of bungling and "simply no justification" for the shooting death of Vicki Weaver. However, the report also criticized Randy Weaver, pointing out that had Weaver gone to court to face charges against him, "his wife and son and a deputy United States Marshal would still be alive today."[3]

Certainly members of militant militia groups and other extremists do not agree with such an assessment. In addition, many Americans who are not extremists were disgusted and even outraged that three deaths occurred because of ineptness by federal authorities. Still they also were likely to concur with one woman living near Ruby Ridge. At the time of siege she said she thought Weaver was dumb for not going to court, and that the feds were "dumb for pressuring him."[4]

The Branch Davidians in Waco

After Ruby Ridge another major tragedy incited militia and other extremists. Members of armed militias—by their statements, publications, and broadcasts—seemed obsessed with the federal authorities' role in the disaster that killed members of a cult known as Branch Davidians. The Davidians, led by David Koresh, lived in a compound near Waco, Texas, called Mount Carmel. Koresh later changed the name to Ranch Apocalypse.

Like Weaver, Koresh was wanted on weapons charges. In February 1993 Koresh and his followers were inside their heavily armed compound when ATF agents tried to force the cult leader's surrender. However, a shootout resulted in the death of four federal agents and six of Koresh's guards who were armed with assault weapons.

FBI agents surrounded the complex and made numerous attempts to persuade Koresh to surrender. After a siege that lasted fifty-one days and included an ATF assault on the compound, the Davidian complex was set afire on April 19 by Branch Davidian disciples, according to most accounts of the tragedy. Koresh and eighty-five cult members, including young children, died in the inferno.

To many Americans who watched television coverage of the long siege and the terrible fire that quickly engulfed all the wooden buildings on the complex, the Davidians were primarily responsible for their own deaths. However, federal agents later admitted making mistakes during the siege and the ATF was highly criticized for pursuing the raid.

There are still many unanswered questions about the assault, including whether or not the ATF agents should have postponed their raid since Koresh knew they were planning to invade. Nevertheless, the ATF agents were duty-bound to investigate reports that Koresh and his followers were stockpiling illegal weapons. In the view of columnist Jack Anderson: "David Koresh was no martyr. He was a dangerous man with a gang of foolish disciples. And, like Randy Weaver, Koresh irrationally believed he was not subject to the laws that govern every other citizen and felt he could make his own rules."[5]

Many extremists and armed militia members, however, thought the Waco deaths were just part of a series of government "murders," such as those of the Weavers and Kahl. Watchdogs who monitor extremists say the Waco disaster helped set the stage for another catastrophe two years later. In fact, a video was quickly produced and circulated among the armed militia groups, warning of more Wacos and urging members to arm themselves in defense.

The Oklahoma Bombing

April 19, 1995, was marked on the calendars of some extremist watchdog groups who for several years had been warning about the threats of the armed militia in the United States. Yet the United States Congress and the media paid little if any attention to reports that tens of thousands of Americans, whether aware of it or not, are involved in groups that include members hell-bent on attacking United States government officials or buildings. Some observers were certain that a violent confrontation would take place on the April date. Not only was it the anniversary of the Waco inferno, it was also the date of the 1995 execution of Richard Snell, a Christian Identity leader, who murdered a state policeman and pawnshop owner. In addition, armed militia members who call themselves patriots like to recall that the first shot of the American Revolution was fired on April 19, 1775.

The anniversary incidents were (and still are) a catalyst for militant militia anger. Yet Americans could hardly imagine the horror that did occur. The nation— indeed, much of the world—was shocked on April 19, 1995, when news of the terrorist bombing of the Alfred P. Murrah Federal Building in Oklahoma City was broadcast.

In the days that followed the Oklahoma City bombing, the count of dead rose to a total of 169 people; hundreds more were injured. Timothy McVeigh and Terry Nichols were arrested in connection with the crime, and speculation mounted regarding the role of an armed militia. Both McVeigh and Nichols had contact

41

with a militant militia group in Michigan. Along with what appeared to be a planned attack on the second anniversary of Waco, the bombing apparently was related to the fact that the federal building housed an office of ATF—a special target for extremist hatred. In addition, McVeigh avidly read *The Turner Diaries,* a 1978 novel by neo-Nazi William Pierce. The book "describes in detail how a truck containing an enormous fertilizer and fuel oil bomb blows up the FBI headquarters at 9:15 in the morning, signaling the beginning of all-out war against the U.S. government." This was just one of numerous parallels between Pierce's bombing description and the Oklahoma City explosion, which the SPLC pointed out in a 1995 report.[6]

Militia members have different views about who is to blame for the Oklahoma City bombing and how it happened. The internet, faxes, phone messages, and talk radio have been filled with countless conspiracy theories. None of them are based on concrete evidence, but they are often believed by people suspicious of the United States government. Some say that the Japanese government planned and carried out the bombing, or that the ADL is responsible, or even that Queen Elizabeth conspired to accomplish the deed. One theorist suggested that the bomb was radioactive and was invented by someone named Riconosciuto.

A frequent story is that the World Trade Center bombing in New York and the bombing of the federal building were connected and part of an FBI plot that includes the two suspected bombers who are government-controlled "zombies." Yet a grand jury found no government conspiracy and charged that McVeigh and Nichols

> did knowingly, intentionally, willfully and maliciously conspire, combine and agree together and with others unknown to the Grand Jury to use a weapon of mass destruction, namely an explosive bomb placed in a truck [a "truck bomb"], against persons within the United States and against property that was owned and used by the United States . . . resulting in death, grievous bodily injury and destruction of the building.[7]

A third defendant, Michael Fortier, was indicted on charges of conspiracy to transport stolen firearms and also was charged with knowingly concealing information about the plan McVeigh and Nichols concocted for bombing the federal building.[8] As part of a plea bargain agreement, Fortier wrote out a confession.

Militia Threats

Linking McVeigh and Nichols with hard-core militia units in Michigan called public attention to the dangers and threats of armed militias. Other high-profile cases involving criminal acts of militia members have also created more public awareness in the 1990s. Yet because of their secretive nature, most armed militias are difficult to monitor. They train in remote places and for the most part do not have highly visible organizations. Some groups deliberately keep their activities hidden by following a leaderless resistance doctrine.

Leaderless resistance has been promoted for years by Louis Beam, a former grand dragon of the Texas Knights

FACTUAL STATEMENT
In Support of Plea Petition

On December 15th and 16th I rode with Tim McVeigh from my home in Kingman, AZ to Kansas. There I was to receive weapons that Tim McVeigh told me had been stolen by Terry Nichols and himself. While in Kansas, McVeigh and I loaded about twenty-five weapons into a car that I had rented. On December 17th, 1994, I drove the rental car back to Arizona through Oklahoma and Oklahoma City. Later, after returning to Arizona and at the request of Tim McVeigh, I sold some of the weapons and again at the request of Tim McVeigh I gave him some money to give to Terry Nichols.

Prior to April 1995, McVeigh told me about the plans that he and Terry Nichols had to blow up the Federal Building in Oklahoma City, Oklahoma. I did not as soon as possible make known my knowledge of the McVeigh and Nichols plot to any judge or other persons in civil authority. When F.B.I. agents questioned me later, about two days after the bombing, and during the next three days, I lied about my knowledge and concealed information. For example, I falsely stated that I had no knowledge of plans to bomb the federal building.

I also gave certain items that I had received from McVeigh, including a bag of ammonium nitrate fertilizer, to a neighbor of mine so the items would not be found by law enforcement officers in a search of my residence.[9]

of the KKK, who spouts anti-Semitic views. During the early 1980s, Beam led the military arm of the Texas Klan, which trained hundreds (some estimate over 2,000) paramilitary soldiers in secret camps. On behalf of white fishermen, these troops intimidated and drove off Vietnamese-American fishermen who were trying to earn a living on the Texas Gulf Coast.

In 1987, after being charged in a plot to overthrow the United States government, Beam fled to Mexico and was on the FBI's "Ten Most Wanted List." He eventually returned to the United States and was tried and acquitted in 1988, apparently because there was not enough evidence to convict him.

To further the objectives of antigovernment groups,

Michigan militia members attend a pro-gun rally in Lansing, Michigan, on September 25, 1994.

45

Beam proposed a phantom cell system—small secret committees—based upon an organization that "does not have a central control or direction." Beam patterned the system after theories publicized in 1962 by Colonel Ulius Louis Amoss, an anti-communist who died in the 1980s.

In an article Beam published in the final issue of the *Seditionist* (February 1992), he notes that Amoss developed his theories because he feared a communist takeover of the United States. Beam adds, "Communism now represents a threat to no one in the United States, while federal tyranny represents a threat to *everyone.*"

Beam explains how groups can resist this so-called tyranny by organizing in a manner just the opposite of the familiar pyramid, with leaders at the top and the masses below. Pyramid organizations are "extremely dangerous for . . . a resistance movement," he states, because "they are easy prey for government infiltration, entrapment, and destruction of the personnel involved." Beam advises antigovernment groups to develop a cell system that has no specified leader. It is a structure that "in the past, many political groups (both right and left) have used . . . to further their objectives," he writes.

With the cell system, small individual groups (cells) operate independently, but cooperate and communicate with each other through newsletters, computers, and other media, "allowing for a planned response" to fight what Beam and his ilk believe is federal oppression.[10]

Leaderless resistance strategy or some variation of it has been adopted by militias in such states as Colorado, Florida, Kansas, Missouri, Texas, and Utah. A version of the resistance structure, a network of underground cells, also has been developed by the Militia of Montana (MOM), one of the most notorious extremist groups.

MOM is based in the northwestern part of the state and has often promoted the views of its leader, John Trochmann, who is known for his ties with the neo-Nazi Aryan Nations. In 1994 Trochmann predicted that a destructive event would take place on April 19, 1995, according to United States Senator Max Baucus of Montana. Senator Baucus testified before a Senate subcommittee that held hearings in mid-1995 to investigate terrorism and the militia. Since militias have formed in Montana "terrorist acts and anti-Semitic incidents have become noticeably more frequent," Baucus said.[11]

Militias in the neighboring state of Idaho have also been in the public eye. Some members of Idaho militias have links with the Aryan Nations headquartered near Hayden Lake. In addition, some Idaho politicians have supported militias. One is United States Representative Helen Chenoweth, who has often expressed sympathy for the militia movement, insisting that it is one way people can protect themselves. After the Oklahoma bombing, Chenoweth said the tragedy indicated there were problems within the federal and state government. The *Idaho Statesman* roundly condemned her in an editorial, calling her a poster child for such groups.

Property Rights Issues

Chenoweth's support of militias in her state stems to some extent from property rights issues, which have sparked bitter debates over many decades in the

American West, especially in rural areas. Private property rights and "takings" of private property by the federal government are a major driving force for the militia movement. Local, state, or federal government can legally "take" private property for public use (such as for a school or post office), provided that the owner is paid a fair price for his or her property. In fact, the Fifth Amendment to the United States Constitution assures that private property cannot "be taken for public use without just compensation." However, some advocates of private property rights, like Chenoweth, say that the "takings" clause, as it is sometimes called, requires the government to pay for expenses a land owner incurs because of environmental laws, such as legislation protecting wetlands or prohibitions against pollution of land and water.

Environmental laws are designed to benefit the larger society, but may sometimes cause economic hardship for an individual land owner. So some land-rights defenders say they have the God-given right to do whatever they want with their own land. They argue as well that the Fifth Amendment is "proof" that the government cannot pass laws regulating land use.

Many land-rights advocates are part of the Wise Use Movement, a coalition of groups against most environmental protection laws and advocates for private use of public lands. The movement was initiated by anti-regulation zealots who corrupted the wise-use ideas of Gifford Pinchot, the first chief of the United States Forest Service. In 1907 Pinchot declared that natural resources such as forests should be used wisely and conserved for future generations. Some Wise Use activists, including cattle ranchers, timber company owners, miners, and others, believe that public lands, such as national parks and wildlife refuges, should be open to private use or development. Actually, that has been true in some cases for many years, especially in the West. Individuals rent public property at very low fees for cattle grazing, mining, logging, and other business enterprises. Theoretically these lands belong to all Americans who pay taxes so that various federal agencies, such as the Bureau of Land Management and the Forest

In the West, some cattle ranchers are able to rent public lands, such as national parks and wildlife refuges, at low fees for cattle grazing. Faced with attempts to increase leasing rates on public lands, many ranchers, miners, and loggers have joined militias in order to fight the federal government and protect their way of earning a living.

Service, can manage them for the public good. Yet those few who use the land to make a profit for their own enterprises reap most of the benefits.[12]

Over the decades numerous attempts have been made to increase leasing rates on public lands. However, ranchers, miners, and others adamantly oppose higher fees and laws restricting what development can take place. They may join militant groups such as armed militias to stage protests. In Catron County, New Mexico, for example, some loggers and ranchers formed a militia because they felt they had to protect their property rights and fight the federal government in order to continue to earn a living. Kenneth Stern reports:

> One rancher insisted that his family had grazed cattle on public land since the Civil War, and that he would continue to use Forest Service land for his 150 head, although he had lost his permit for ignoring an order not to send his cattle into an area that had been burned and reseeded. The Forest Service and the Bureau of Land Management had the authority to impound such cattle—which were, after all, trespassing on and harming public land.

However, federal officials have done little to stop such lawbreakers. Forest Service employees in Catron County and their families, including their children, have been threatened, and officials fear that their agents will be injured or killed.[13]

Common Beliefs

Over and over again the message of militant militias (as well as others opposed to government regulations) is

Many members of militant militias believe that federal government agents in black helicopters are flying around the United States to spy on citizens, especially Patriots.

clear: the federal government is the enemy. Yet that is not the only common thread. Besides their belief that the Oklahoma City bombing was part of a federal government plot to justify arresting or killing militia members, they share other convictions. If they are followers of Christian Identity preachers, they say that taking lives is warranted as retribution for the "evils" of the federal government. Even if members do not condone murder, they are likely to have ideas such as these in common:

- Federal government agents in black helicopters are flying around the United States, spying on citizens, especially Patriots, to prepare for the New

51

World Order and the United Nations (UN) takeover of the country.

- Coded markings have been placed on the backs of road signs to guide UN forces.

- Various kinds of foreign troops are being trained in sites across the United States.

- Trains and ships docked in the United States are carrying foreign military supplies in preparation for the New World Order.

- The Israeli government controls the United States government.

- The anti-terrorism law, enacted in April 1996 in order to combat incidents like the Oklahoma City bombing, is designed to revoke the United States Constitution.

- News broadcasters and newspaper publishers refuse to inform the American people about the conspiracy information gathered by the militia because the news media are part of the overall conspiracy.

- Weather is being controlled by the federal government in order to destroy people and property with earthquakes, floods, and other disasters.

Conspiracy beliefs, which seem unreasonable and even absurd to many Americans, are well entrenched with militant militias. The danger is that these beliefs could be the catalyst for armed resistance or even civil war.

5

Gun Owners and
the Militia

Millions of law-abiding Americans own guns, but they have no intention of waging a civil war against their government. Some use their guns for sports, such as hunting and target practice, or keep their guns for self-defense. Many belong to national organizations that support their interests. The most well-known is the National Rifle Association (NRA), founded more than one hundred years ago by sports enthusiasts. Today the NRA is often depicted as an organization primarily concerned with opposing gun-control laws.

NRA's Hostility
In recent years NRA leaders have issued numerous hostile statements against gun control and federal law enforcement that give the impression that the organization sides with armed militias. But NRA leaders claim the organization has become a scapegoat—has been unjustly blamed for unlawful militia activities. As

the NRA's Executive Vice President Wayne LaPierre declared at a 1995 convention, "We don't train for a revolt in the woods; we train for safety. We don't break the laws; we help make the laws."[1]

Although numerous public officials support the NRA, some politicians have denounced the organization and its leadership, particularly for its 1995 fund-raising letter, signed by LaPierre. In the letter, LaPierre more than once called law enforcement agents "jackbooted government thugs." He cited tragic incidents such as Ruby Ridge and Waco, claiming that "not too long ago, it was unthinkable for Federal agents wearing Nazi bucket helmets and black storm trooper uniforms to attack law-abiding citizens."[2]

The letter, or portions of it, were circulated widely in print and broadcast media, prompting former President George Bush to write to Thomas L. Washington, then president of the NRA. Bush was especially outraged with LaPierre's implication that American law enforcement agents were comparable to Nazis, calling it "a vicious slander on good people." President Bush noted that he had long "agreed with most of NRA's objectives," but the organization's "broadside against Federal agents deeply offends my own sense of decency and honor and it offends my concept of service to country. It indirectly slanders a wide array of government law enforcement officials, who are out there, day and night, laying their lives on the line for all of us."[3] Bush ended his letter with a resignation of his NRA membership.

Other politicians, including California's Governor Pete Wilson, commended Bush's actions. Attorney

General Janet Reno noted that former President Bush had set a powerful example, saying it was "just plain wrong" to spread negative stereotypes of law enforcement officials who were at risk "each day in defense of our freedoms."[4]

What Is the NRA?

Incorporated in 1871, the NRA for years was primarily made up of traditional sportsmen—hunters, target shooters, and gun collectors. Today it has a membership of about 3 million, dropping from its high of 3.5 million members in 1995, and is considered an activist organization that adamantly supports pro-gun politicians. According to an analysis by the Center for Responsive Politics, a nonpartisan research group, the NRA spent $5.3 million in 1994 to support political candidates who were against bans on guns.[5]

"The NRA's political action committee, the Political Victory Fund, is the nation's largest," reports *Mother Jones* magazine, which favors gun control.

> In 1994, this PAC outspent all other groups . . . on behalf of pro-gun candidates, and money for phone banks and mailings to NRA members telling them how to vote. The bulk of that money contributed mightily to the Republican Party's takeover of Congress—79 percent of NRA campaign contributions and 87 percent of the independent expenditures went to the GOP.[6]

NRA leaders have pulled away from the organization's original emphasis on sports shooting and hunting, although most of its members have not. In

1995 the NRA's late president, Tom Washington, said the focus on gun rights was necessary in order to fight legal bans on gun ownership. The new president, Marion Hammer, who took over the office after Washington died in December 1995, has continued that emphasis. She has consistently stressed the NRA's contention that the Second Amendment confers the right of individuals to

Many Americans own guns so that they can participate in sports such as hunting and target practice.

own guns—any kind of guns. At the 1996 NRA convention, Hammer, the first woman to head the organization, told assembled members, "I may be only four foot eleven, but when I stand up for NRA, stand up for our Constitution, and stand up for the Second Amendment, I feel ten feet tall—because I'm standing on the high moral ground of freedom!"[7]

To the NRA, the Second Amendment right "eclipses all others," because the right to own a gun and the power of a firearm defends the individual against an unpredictable government, according to investigative reporter Jack Anderson. In his opinion, most NRA members believe that "a nation forged in armed revolution cannot take lightly the right to keep and bear arms because one never knows when armed revolution could again be necessary. For the NRA, the fight against tyranny never ended."[8]

That fight has included extensive efforts to oppose gun controls through the NRA's Institute for Legislative Action (ILA) headed by Tanya Metaksa. Metaksa is the organization's chief lobbyist in Washington, D.C., and has been responsible for sending numerous letters, faxes, and Internet messages to members with inflammatory words, warning about dangers to their civil rights. She urges them to vote for candidates sympathetic to NRA causes or to deluge Congress with letters and faxes opposing gun controls.

For example, Congress enacted a law in 1993 restricting the manufacture of assault weapons and in 1994 passed legislation known as the Brady Bill, which requires a person to register and wait five days before he or she can purchase a handgun. Metaksa and other NRA leaders lobbied against the laws, insisting that a Great Gun Grab was about to take place.[9] As columnist Jack Anderson stated: "To the NRA leadership there is no distinction between reasonable and limited restrictions on gun purchase and ownership on the one hand, and confiscation of all the arms owned by the American people on the other."[10]

NRA's Position on Militias

While there is little doubt that the NRA supports unrestricted gun ownership, many Americans have questioned the organization's position on armed militias. The NRA has become suspect because of revelations that some of its members are also members of paramilitary groups advocating violence against the federal government. Of course, no organization is responsible for the behavior of all its members, but the NRA has supported people who advocate armed militia action against the federal government.

In 1995, for instance, the organization named then-Sheriff Richard Mack of Graham County, Arizona, its Law Enforcement Officer of the Year. Mack said he "wouldn't hesitate for a minute to call out my posse against the federal government if it gets out of hand."[11] The NRA also provided $25,000 in funds to aid Mack in his lawsuit against the federal government "to avoid enforcement of the Brady Law, an action that has earned him the admiration of militiamen nationwide," according to a report in *USA Today* magazine.[12] Mack was defeated in a 1996 primary election for sheriff, perhaps because voters did not like the fact that he was often traveling out of state, addressing various militia and Christian Identity groups. Since his defeat, Mack has been making the rounds of TV and radio talk shows, advocating repeal of gun-control laws.

NRA vs. Armed Militias

After its 1995 convention, the NRA's board of directors prepared a policy statement on armed militias that was released to the media, posted on the Internet, and linked to the NRA's WWW site. In part, it stated:

- The NRA vehemently disavows any connection with, or tacit approval of, any club or individual which advocates (1) the overthrow of duly constituted government authority, (2) subversive activities directed at any government, (3) the establishment or maintenance of private armies or group violence.

- The NRA does not approve or support any group activities that properly belong to the national defense or the police.

- The NRA does not approve or support any group that by force, violence, or subversion seeks to overthrow the Government and take the law into its own hands, or that endorses or espouses doctrines of operation in an extralegal manner.

- The NRA stands squarely on the premise that the ownership of firearms must not be denied American citizens of good repute so long as the firearms are used for lawful purposes.

- The NRA has insisted, does insist, and will continue to insist on the traditional right of American citizens to own and use firearms for lawful purposes. . . .[13]

Young boys hold signs at a pro-gun rally in Lansing, Michigan, on September 25, 1994.

A New Image for NRA Leaders?

Although NRA leaders have tried since the organization's 1995 convention to appear less militant, the NRA is led by individuals such as First Vice President Neal Knox, who is known as "the architect of a revolution that has transformed the group from an organization of hunters and target-shooting sportsmen into a militant faction," in the opinion of *Mother Jones*.

During its 1996 annual gathering, the organization was on the attack against gun control advocates and laws requiring registration for gun ownership. Knox repeated an assertion that he has often made: The Holocaust—the terrible destruction of millions of Jews and others by

German Nazis during World War II—could have been prevented if citizens had been allowed to keep their guns without registering them. In his address to members, Knox claimed that the objective of gun registration laws is "confiscation." He reasoned that "gun registration was used to disarm Germany's Jews, and to disarm the people of occupied lands in Europe. The Holocaust could never have occurred if Germany's Jews had had the means to defend themselves."[14]

The JPFO

Such ideas have been circulated by Jews for the Preservation of Firearms Ownership (JPFO), a radical pro-gun group. According to investigative reporter Jonathan Karl, JPFO was founded in 1989 by Aaron Zelman, a Vietnam veteran and a Milwaukee gun dealer. The organization frequently defends the militia movement, arguing that Adolf Hitler

> . . . began his path to dictatorship and mass murder with gun control. If the Jews in Germany had been armed, JPFO reasons, there would have been no Holocaust. JPFO also argues that every other murderous dictator of the twentieth century . . . consolidated their power through gun control.[15]

In 1994, *Guns & Ammo* magazine published an article by Jay Simkin, the president of JFPO, who stated his belief that genocides could be "prevented if civilians worldwide own[ed] military-type rifles and plenty of ammunition."[16]

Holocaust scholars and researchers as well as other historians find little to support such a theory. The forces that contributed to the mass destruction of Jews and others by Nazis could hardly have been stopped by gun-toting individuals acting on their own, although one threatened person might have been able to effectively protect himself or herself with a weapon.

Gun Owners of America

The Gun Owners of America (GOA), based in Falls Church, Virginia, is another nationwide group of gun owners; membership totals between 150,000 to 200,000. It appears more radical than the JPFO, and its leaders are certainly more militant than those of the NRA.

GOA's director Larry Pratt wrote *Armed Citizens Victorious*, published in 1990, that advocates forming citizen militias. A former Virginia legislator, Pratt was one of the co-chairmen of Pat Buchanan's 1995–96 presidential campaign, but he resigned in February 1996. His resignation followed a report by the Center for Public Integrity (CPI), a nonpartisan research organization focusing on ethics in government. Titled "Under the Influence: The 1996 Presidential Candidates and Their Campaign Advisers," the study revealed that Pratt's beliefs are similar to Christian Patriots and other far-right groups—gun ownership is dictated by the Scripture and that Christians "have a responsibility" to keep and bear arms.[17]

Pratt has also been a featured speaker at meetings of white supremacists and followers of the neo-Nazi Aryan Nations and has written for anti-Semitic magazines. In addition, he has been a guest on a cable TV program whose host is Pete Peters, a preacher of the Christian Identity theology. Pratt espouses the view that "it is time that the United States return to reliance on an armed people. There is no acceptable alternative."[18]

Radical leaders who support arming citizens for civil war have helped promote an antigovernment message, which in turn has helped militias "build their membership and spread their message through gun shows around the country," Kenneth Stern notes in his book on the militias. Unfortunately, this has convinced many militia members that "shooting American public officials is a patriotic duty."[19]

Nevertheless, truly patriotic Americans—most citizens—do not seem to accept the view that owning a gun is a matter of protecting one's civil rights. Polls show that at least 75 percent of Americans favor the ban on assault weapons and a vast majority favor the law that requires a forty-eight hour waiting period for a handgun purchase. Most Americans, in fact, condemn armed militia activities.[20]

6

The Growing Movement

Whatever the support for or condemnation of the militia movement in the United States, some militias abandoned their paramilitary activities after the Oklahoma City bombing. The Oregon Militia dissolved because its founder, Michael J. Cross, said he suspected that agents of the federal government had infiltrated his group. Cross told reporters that he had destroyed all the militia records and instructed members "to form small cell groups" that he declared "would be safer than one big organization."[1]

Militias in other states were forced to disband because of community disapproval of their activities, but they reorganized as educational or political groups or changed their names. For example, the Colorado Militia became the Front Range Patriots and proclaimed that it was not a radical group. Others simply lost some of their membership.

However, as some militias drop out or regroup, there

is little doubt that overall the armed and dangerous militia movement has been expanding in some states. A survey released in 1995 by the Anti-Defamation League showed that although there is no uniform pattern of growth, "militia gains plainly appear to outweigh losses." Militias are "operating in at least 40 states, with membership reaching some 15,000," the ADL reported.[2] In the two years between 1994 and 1996, the SPLC and its Militia Task Force counted at least 441 militia units across the United States and an additional 368 Patriot groups linked with the militias; Patriots promote formation of militias and provide them with information and materials.[3]

The bombing of the federal building, which many Americans thought would turn the spotlight on terrorist militia activities and discourage membership, brought even more people into the militant fold. Some joined militias because they were potential recruits who had never heard about militias but joined because of all the publicity about such groups. Others became militia members because they believed the conspiracy myth that the federal government was responsible for the bombing.

Acting on such beliefs, some armed militia members have targeted other buildings for bombings and have threatened individuals fighting against dangerous militias. One example is the foiled plan of the Oklahoma Constitutional Militia and its leader, Ray Lampley, to blow up a number of buildings in November 1995.

Thanks to quick work by the FBI, the plan failed and Lampley, his wife Cecilia, and associates Larry Wayne Crow and J. D. Baird were arrested and charged with

Members of a white supremacist group called the White Patriot Party in North Carolina wear military garb and recruit members from the military, an illegal activity.

plotting to blow up the Southern Poverty Law Center, offices of the ADL, abortion clinics, and gay bars. They were arrested while preparing explosives "made of ammonium nitrate, nitromethane, aluminum powder and a detonation device," according to the criminal complaint brought against them in a United States District Court in Oklahoma.[4] This recipe could have created "an explosive force of 17,389 feet of force per second," according to SPLC legal counsel Morris Dees.

He states that the staff's close call with death only made them "more determined than ever to continue our work."[5]

Hate Messages

Although not all militia groups are militant and dangerous, many are led or influenced by people who spew their venom, frequently espousing anti-Semitic and white supremacist views. Most of these leaders deny they are against Jews and people of color and call themselves separatists, but their words and deeds clearly show their bigotry as well as their readiness to commit terrorist acts.

Pete Peters of Laramie, Wyoming, fits that profile. Peters is a self-styled minister of the Laporte, Colorado, Church of Christ, which is based on Christian Identity ideas. He has published numerous hate materials that are distributed across the United States and posted on the Internet. After the Oklahoma City bombing, he spoke to a group of Identity and Patriot followers who had gathered in Branson, Missouri, showing no sympathy whatsoever for victims of the bombing. Instead, he railed against the federal government, claiming as other radical leaders have done, that the deaths were part of a plot to turn the public against paramilitary groups. Peters prayed for delivery "from the anti-Christ enemies who plot against us; strike them down! . . . Keep us, your people Israel, safe from your enemy, the anti-Christs who have done this thing and put it on us, your people!"[6]

Long before this tirade, Peters had preached his Christian Identity theology that encourages followers to be militant. He told believers that they can lawfully (according to Identity law) and with a clear conscience kill those they believe are subhuman or children of Satan.[7]

In October 1992 Peters, reacting to the siege at Ruby Ridge, orchestrated a gathering at Estes Park, Colorado, and called for paramilitary groups to organize. Some observers believe this meeting initiated the current militia movement in the United States.

However, Kenneth Stern noted in his book on the militia that Eva Vail Lamb had started the Idaho Organized Militia months before the Estes Park meeting. Also, in the spring of 1992, James "Bo" Gritz, who was the anti-Semitic Populist Party candidate for United States president and part of the negotiating team seeking the surrender of Randy Weaver, had called on his supporters to form militias. Gritz has since conducted "survivalist—some say paramilitary—training" that he calls Specially Prepared Individuals for Key Events (SPIKE).[8] In addition, Gritz has set up a community called Almost Heaven in Kamiah, Idaho—a haven for survivalists—who often are supporters or members of paramilitary groups.

In Montana, John Trochmann, his brother David, and his nephew Randy, who cofounded the Militia of Montana (MOM) in 1993, have distributed conspiracy propaganda that warns against a New World Order. John Trochmann has written most of the materials he publishes, including training manuals for paramilitary groups. He travels extensively to speak, urging his audiences to take up arms and hide out in the hills, mountains, and other isolated areas.

Accused of being aligned with the hate group Aryan Nations, John Trochmann always denies this association. Yet the Aryan Nations responded with a statement saying Trochmann had attended Bible studies and even helped "write a set of rules for our code of conduct on the church grounds." Trochmann also told a member of the Sanders County Task Force for Human Dignity, which formed to oppose militia activities, that when MOM and other militias take over, the task force member "would never be able to stay in America" because he's Italian.[9]

Other Radical Leaders

Other radical leaders who express views similar to Trochmann's include Reverend Norman Olson, a Baptist minister and gunshop owner, and one of his parishioners, Ray Southwell. In 1994 Olson, who calls himself a Brigadier General, and Southwell cofounded a regional militia group that eventually became the Michigan Militia.

With the help of Ken Adams, who was once communications director for the Michigan Militia, Olson and Southwell sought and gained a great deal of publicity for their views. They have appeared on TV talk shows and have been quoted extensively by news reporters. When they issued a press release in May 1995 blaming the Japanese government for the Oklahoma City bombing, Olson and Southwell were forced to resign from the Michigan Militia because of complaints from members.

Nevertheless, Olson has continued to make himself heard. In testimony before a United States Senate hearing on terrorism, Olson repeated the claim so often used by people in the militia movement that "the fundamental function of the militia in society remains with the people." He told the Senate committee:

> While some say that the right to keep and bear arms is granted to Americans by the Constitution, just the opposite is true. The Federal Government itself is the child of the armed citizen. We the people are the parent of the child we call government. You, Senators, are part of the child that We The People gave life to. The increasing amount of Federal encroachment into our lives indicates the need for parental corrective action. In short, the Federal government needs a good spanking to make it behave.[10]

Another group in Michigan not affiliated with the

Ray Southwell cofounded a regional militia group that eventually became the Michigan Militia.

Michigan Militia is led by activist Mark Koernke of Dexter. Koernke founded a secretive group called the Michigan Militia-at-Large, although he himself does not shy away from publicity. Like Trochmann, he travels extensively to speak and distributes his tapes and videos nationwide to proclaim his message about the evils of government. In a movie he produced titled *America in Peril,* he appears with a rope and rifle, telling his audience that "you can get about four politicians for about 120 foot of rope. . . . Remember, whenever using it, always try and find a willow tree. The entertainment will last longer."[11]

In the neighboring state of Indiana, another radical, Joe Holland, founded the North American Volunteer Militia, as well as an organization called the Freedom Council and one known as the Bill of Rights Enforcement Center. Holland operated a pig farm in Booneville, and refused to pay taxes on the farm. The farm was eventually seized and sold by the IRS to pay income taxes that Holland owed. According to an Internet report in the Militia Watchdog, Holland, like other common-law advocates, promoted fake money orders that were sold in amounts up to $500.

> One typical use of such money orders was to fill out the amount with a figure twice the sum owed to a person or organization, then ask for an immediate refund of the "overpayment." If the person receiving the money order suspected nothing and wrote out a check for the "overpayment," he or she would be very unhappily surprised when the bank refused to deposit the money order. Joe Holland, who regularly sold such money orders, claimed that they were a method

of protest rather than a scam. "Congress has sold you out," he claimed. "They have given up their authority to produce your money. The money order brings the issue to the forefront."[12]

Holland continued his anti-tax activities, linking with another radical, Calvin Greenup of Montana, who called government agents "predators." The pair began a letter-writing and fax campaign that predicted a "full-scale civil war" and warned that "people of this country are sick and tired of being raped and pillaged by the bunch of thieves that run the federal government." Then in December 1994 Holland wrote to the Montana Revenue Department and in his letter boasted that he was

> . . . the leader of the nation's largest militia, capable of mobilizing a million people, and asked "How many of your agents will be sent home in body bags before you hear the pleas of the people? Proceed at your own peril!"

In May 1995 Holland mailed a letter to 12,000 registered voters of Ravalli County in Montana, attacking the judge who had ordered Holland's extradition to Montana. He accused the judge of misconduct. The tactic

> . . . constituted an act of jury tampering, as Holland had mailed letters to the entire jury pool of Ravalli County. In addition, one of the others against whom charges had been brought pleaded guilty and agreed to testify against Holland. In late May, Holland finally agreed to be extradited to Montana, where he faced the possibility of up to 20 years in prison and a $50,000 fine.

He eventually pled guilty but was allowed to go free, pending an appeals trial.[13]

One other rabble-rouser in Indiana is Linda Thompson of Indianapolis, a lawyer who once was a pro-choice activist, working for pregnant women who chose to have an abortion. During the Waco siege she traveled to Texas and became an advocate for David Koresh, calling for people to take up arms. "JOIN US!" she urged in a press release. "The Unorganized Militia of the United States of America will assemble, with long arms, vehicles (including tracked and armored), aircraft, and any gear for inspection for fitness and use in a well-regulated militia, at 9:00 A.M. on Saturday, April 3, 1993, on Norcrest Drive, off I-35."[14]

Although she was unable to organize the militia at that time, Thompson soon set up a computer bulletin board service—a means of communicating by posting messages on a computer through a telephone hookup and Internet access. She also produced a videotape called *Waco: The Big Lie,* and later, *Waco II: The Big Lie Continues.* As the titles suggest, the videos vilify government actions in Waco and emphasize conspiracy theories. In fact, the videos have helped popularize the theories among militias and fostered the idea that the Branch Davidians were deliberately murdered by government agents.[15]

In 1994 Thompson called for an armed militia to march on Washington, D.C., to arrest members of Congress whom she considered "traitors." But the march was canceled due to what she labeled a "CIA conspiracy plot" against her.

Influential as she once was, Thompson, who calls herself the Adjutant General of the Unorganized Militia, seems to have faded from the public scene. She still heads the American Justice Federation, established in 1993 to circulate materials about the militia and conspiracy theories. In 1994 the federation circulated a document called a "Declaration of Independence by the Sovereign Citizens of the Several States Within the United States of America." The declaration uses paragraphs from the original Declaration of Independence adopted in 1776 by the Continental Congress, but it makes accusations against the "present federal government of the United States of America."

Spreading the Militia Doctrine

A major factor in the growth of militias is communication. Groups can widely circulate their views through a variety of means. Many militia leaders publish their propaganda in such magazines as *Aid & Abet, Taking Aim, Guns & Ammo,* and *Soldier of Fortune.* Militias have established fax networks to quickly send out newsletters, bulletins, and articles. They also use the Internet, setting up World Wide Web (WWW) pages to distribute their views. In mid-1996 several WWW sites operated by militia members were even distributing copies of a book titled *Report from Iron Mountain,* which mocks the idea that countries must wage war in order to prosper.

First published in 1967, the book was reissued in 1996 by Simon & Schuster with a statement clearly noting that *Iron Mountain* is a satire. Since its distribution throughout 1996 on WWW sites maintained by militias, *Iron Mountain* has become "a classic" for militia members because they believe it is an authentic report, according to *The New York Times*.

The idea for *Iron Mountain* was conceived by Victor Navasky, Richard Lingeman, and Leonard C. Lewin as a political parody. It mimics "a leaked government report supposedly delivered to Mr. Lewin by one of the 15 members of a special government group. But in 1972, Mr. Lewin publicly announced that he was the real author of the report, a hoax he said was created to raise issues of war and peace in a provocative way," the *Times* reported.[16]

While pirating of this book has virtually stopped on the Internet due to threatened lawsuits, other types of propaganda appear, such as that shown on the Web site of the Constitutional Militia of Southern California. Its home page states that it serves "The Citizens of the Entire State of California" and carries the banner: "Join the ARMY—Serve the United Nations. Join the MILITIA—Serve AMERICA!" Like most militia home pages on the Internet, there is a quote from the Second Amendment. The page also warns that "Today, the militia are demonized by the media, and scrutinized by the government. Many Patriots are now useing [sic] PGP data encryption."[17] (PGP stands for Pretty Good Privacy, a program to code information for privacy.)

The Southern California Militia also takes great pains to describe its membership. With a link to the document "Who Are We?" the response, as posted, states in part:

> Contrary to what you may have read in the newspapers, or heard on the radio, or even seen on

the television news, we are not a group of "goose-stepping" anti-Semitic racists with single digit IQ's. And in spite of what the government, and its lackeys in the media would have you believe, we are not a bunch of mad-bombers. We are not out to destroy the government. We are hoping to restore it.

. . . We are Patriots, sworn to protect and defend the Constitution of the United States of America against all enemies both foreign and domestic.

. . . We are your neighbor, your secretary, your doctor, the mechanic who fixed your car. . . . We are Americans.[18]

Some WWW sites maintained by militia members carry spiteful criticism of groups opposed to armed militias. The Lee County Militia/1st Florida Regiment/1st U. S. Militia goes one ugly step further by associating monitoring groups with what it calls "Links to National Socialist (NAZI) Propoganda [sic] and other Enemies of the People." It includes Universal Resource Locators (URLs), or "addresses," for access to ADL materials and the Militia Watchdog home page, as examples, along with neo-Nazi home pages like that of the Aryan Nations. With these links is the warning: "Carefull [sic], Some of these devils are pretty smooth talkers, and defend their dogma with religious fever [sic]."[19]

Recruiting for the Militia in the Military

The military also appears to be fertile ground for militia recruiters. Since the late 1980s, there have been a number of incidents indicating that members of the United States military have joined groups such as the White Patriot Party of North Carolina, created by a former Green Beret, Glenn Miller, who was intent on starting a war against blacks, Jews, and the federal government.

In 1991 three Green Berets at Fort Bragg were arrested and two were convicted in a plot that involved stealing weapons for a race war. Four years later, in 1995, two white solders shot and killed an African-American couple after harassing them while they were walking down the street. Although there is no clear proof that the Fort Bragg incidents were connected with militias, an army investigation has found that out of tens of thousands of soldiers, a small percentage hold extremist views.

The New York Times reported in March 1996 that "Senior Army commanders believe that members of the Special Operations Forces, the elite fighting units that include the Green Berets, have been selected for recruitment by extremist militias." In its report, the army noted that evidence was lacking to "confirm or deny this belief," but in a survey of 17,080 soldiers, the army "found that 3.5 percent of them had been approached to join an extremist organization since joining the Army, while another 7.1 percent reported that they knew another soldier who was probably a member of an extremist group."[20]

Broadcasting Propaganda

Radio and cable TV are also media for militia recruiting and propaganda. Ken Adams, former publicity director for the Michigan Militia, is known for his weekly radio show "Take America Back." Now head of a group called the National Confederation of Citizen Militias, Adams

Since the late 1980s, extremist militias have often met with success in their attempts to recruit members of the United States military.

claims his talk show, which is broadcast nationwide, is not specifically for militias. Yet that is the topic often covered by callers, and Adams reportedly "uses his show and other communication tools—faxes, the Internet—to act as liaison among militia organizations."[21]

Adams's show and other broadcasts, such as those conducted by shortwave radio enthusiast William Cooper of Arizona, often focus on the popular one world conspiracy theories as well as the ideas in the anti-Semitic *Protocols of the Learned Elders of Zion.* Such myths continue to circulate not only among the radical groups but also throughout some mainstream talk radio and TV.

Modern communication methods can spread information in minutes, and it is easy to call into a talk show to pass on an outlandish rumor about, for example, a truck full of guillotines that supposedly will be used by Jewish conspirators to behead Christians who are Patriots. Another story circulated in 1995 on shortwave radio when Ben McKnight of Texas repeated an oft-told myth that detention centers were set up across the United States to hold militia members. He also told of a plane full of United States military officers who were bound and gagged, reportedly seen by an unnamed witness.[22]

These and other absurd stories become believable to listeners who do little critical thinking and do not question the truthfulness of the source or the lack of evidence behind what they hear. To counteract radical militia propaganda, numerous Americans are rallying against ideas based on fear, prejudice, and myth and the belief that citizens have to arm themselves in order to protect their civil rights. Some are acting on the proposition that extremism is not the answer to government problems. Rather, they urge people to reject radicals and rabble-rousers. One woman in Montana, who was quoted in Stern's book on the militia, put it this way: "I think our whole country should be afraid of what they [the militia] are creating . . . a situation where the federal government has to get tougher. . . . It's madness." She went on to warn against citizen apathy.[23]

This woman is certainly not alone in the call for individuals to be informed about the armed and dangerous militias. Some citizens have already begun to speak out, to be, as President Bill Clinton said at a town meeting in Montana, "a vigorous voice of citizen responsibility."[24] In addition, watchdog groups continue to monitor militia and patriot activities.

7

Watchdogs

While there are nationally known and active militia watchdog groups, such as the ADL and the SPLC's Militia Task Force, citizen groups also are forming to counter or protest armed militia intimidation. Likewise, some political leaders are urging action to counter paramilitary activities. However, proposed laws at the federal level to ban or restrict paramilitary groups have met with stiff opposition not only from within the militia movement and among gun owners, but also from those who fear that civil liberties will be violated.

Citizen Action

Since the early 1990s in Montana, where the militia movement is strong, some church leaders have set up special offices and projects to "offset the movement's racist, anti-Semitic and antigovernment messages," according to the *National Catholic Reporter.* Because white supremacists and leaders of the militia movement foresee Montana and other Northwest states as a "white republic," the Montana Association of Churches (MAC) has organized a project to counter their ideology, specifically Christian Identity theology.

Margaret McDonald, director of MAC, believes that people have to talk about the racist attitudes of some militia leaders so they will be prepared "to take public action in solidarity with people who are targeted." Otherwise, she contends, the situation can become like that of Nazi Germany in the 1920s and 1930s when it was "too frightening for good folks to speak out. People need to be witnesses in a public way," she stated.[1]

In Helena, Montana, another group that is part of the Montana Anti-Extremist Coalition gathered on April 19, 1996, the anniversary of the Oklahoma City bombing, to protest armed extremists. They also kicked off a petition drive to place on the ballot an initiative (a proposed law initiated by the people) to counter antigovernment militants.

One section of the initiative would allow anyone threatened by militants to sue for monetary damages. In a National Public Radio "NewsHour" show, Evan Barrett, who leads the ballot drive, said that:

> Silence is consent, and if we stand by silent in the face of this kind of extremism, those who perpetrate that kind of violence and activity will believe that we're on their side, and most mainstream America and mainstream Montana is not on the side of those who would perpetrate violence.

Don Judge of the coalition noted: "We abhor the vilification of government workers as a threat to people and an assault on our democracy, and we urge all Montanans to stand up and be counted against the acts of political hatred and division."[2]

Early in 1996, a group in Washington State called the Whatcom (County) Human Rights Task Force sent out a news release expressing concern about a scheduled speech by John Trochmann of MOM. The task force contacted community groups in Whatcom and adjacent Skagit County to inform them about the Militia of Montana and to explain why they opposed "armed vigilante groups." Vernon Johnson, co-chair of the WHRTF, stressed that group members "believe in free speech and freedom of association," but that the community needed "to be informed about where . . . [militia] movements are really coming from." In its news release, the WHRTF charged that:

- The promoters of armed vigilante groups spread fear and intimidation by their aggressive posturing about "enemies." This stifles public discussion of real issues and makes people fearful of making their views known.

- The irresponsible and untrue conspiracy theories promoted by Trochmann and others turn people's concerns about real issues into fear-mongering and paranoia.

- The use of armed vigilante groups to confront federal authority has roots in the racist movement. Racist groups like the Posse Comitatus and the Committee of the States advocated forming "unorganized militias" during the previous two decades. Many leaders of the current movement have long-standing connections to the white supremacy movement.[3]

Along with its warning to communities, the task force announced its plan for a project called Joining Hands Against Hate. Throughout the month of January 1996, WHRTF encouraged people to display a poster of joined hands. The symbol was a way for residents to show they would not let fear and intolerance rule their lives and that they supported efforts to live together peacefully and safely.

Group Action

Reports from well-known groups that monitor armed militias have appeared in numerous newspapers and news magazines in recent years. However, other groups, which might not be as familiar to the general public, are disseminating information on militia threats through various media, including Internet postings.

Political Research Associates (PRA), for example, which was founded in Chicago in 1981, is a clearinghouse for information on racist and anti-democratic right-wing political groups. Now based in Cambridge, Massachusetts, PRA maintains a library, supports a small publishing enterprise, and provides speakers for conferences, seminars, and classes. PRA analyst Chip Berlet often posts articles about armed militia activities on the Internet and encourages distribution of the information.

People Against Racist Terror (PART) in Burbank, California, produces numerous reports on racism and anti-Semitic and anti-Arab activities, and recently issued

Members of an Arizona militia sharpen their shooting skills in the desert. Many militia members like these have formed secret cells. This is an especially dangerous development in the "Patriot" world because the secret cells are difficult to monitor and can strike when least expected.

a report, "Reactionary Forces Link Up in Militias," that is available for reading and downloading on the Internet. It includes access to descriptions of various groups linked to armed militias and can be found at http://www.igc.apc.org.

The Institute for Alternative Journalism sponsors a Democracy Works home page that can be accessed by a link at http://www.igc.apc.org. This page includes a list of groups and WWW sites that promote democracy and diversity, and monitor armed militia groups. Monitoring groups include the Institute for First Amendment Studies, Militia Watchdog, Public Good, and Radio for Peace International. Mailing addresses for these and other groups are listed at the back of this book.

The Coalition for Human Dignity (CHD) also has a web site. It can be accessed at http://www.chdseattle.org/chd/. Founded in 1988, CHD "is dedicated to strengthening democracy and defending civil rights," the organization states on its home page. CHD helps communities respond to organized threats from armed militias and other groups spreading racist, anti-Semitic, and homophobic ideas. Reports that can be accessed at the site include a ground-breaking document on extremist activities in the Pacific Northwest titled *The Northwest Imperative: Documenting a Decade of Hate.*

In July 1995 CHD helped bring together a panel to testify before members of the United States House of Representatives. The panel included "officials, activists and citizens who have been targets of militia and 'Patriot' harassment and violence," reported Jonathan Mozzochi, executive director of CHD.[4]

A few months later, in November 1995, at the request of Representative Charles Schumer of New York, the United States House of Representatives Committee on the Judiciary, Subcommittee on Crime, held hearings on violent antigovernment groups. When Schumer addressed the committee, he warned that "armed radical groups . . . are a sickness of hate, paranoia, and violence" that threatens "our future as a free country." He accused extremists of assaulting "democracy by choosing the bomb and the bullet over the ballot box."[5]

Schumer said he supported the right of people to belong to militias and "to debate and to advocate even the most radical theories of government." Yet he called for "firm action against the violence that erupts from these groups." The congressman introduced a bill that he said would curb violent actions, and also noted that "every American must take a stand against them" or America will be destroyed.[6]

More Laws?

More than forty states have laws that ban the formation of armed militias or paramilitary training or prohibit both, but states do not necessarily enforce these laws. Some local officials fear (justifiably so) they will be targets of militia intimidation or be shot by those they try to arrest. Another reason for lack of enforcement is that some police, along with various state officials and United States Representatives, support militias, and their views could have an influence on whether or not enforcement agencies do their job.

Congressman Steve Stockman of Houston, Texas, is an outspoken advocate of militias and was elected from his district by those who agree with his stance. In 1995 he wrote a letter to Attorney General Janet Reno, stating, in part, that "a number of reliable sources" (which turned out to be otherwise) had informed him there would be a raid on March 25 or 26

> . . . by several Federal agencies, against the "citizen's militias" groups. . . . A paramilitary style attack

against Americans who pose no risk to others, even if violations of criminal law might be imputed to them, would run the risk of an irreparable breach between the Federal government and the public.[7]

No raid took place, and the sources of Stockman's information turned out to be based on rumors posted on the Internet and spread through faxes by militia groups. Stockman's support of armed militias also was evident in an article he wrote for the June 1995 issue of *Guns & Ammo* magazine. According to ADL's 1995 report on the militia, Stockman claimed:

> The raid on the Branch Davidian compound in Waco was conducted by the Clinton Administration "to prove the need for a ban on so-called assault weapons." Earlier, Stockman appeared as a guest on the radio program of Liberty Lobby, the leading anti-Semitic propaganda group in the nation; he has since said he was unaware of Liberty Lobby's anti-Semitism.[8]

At the state level, Colorado State Senator Charles Duke is an avid supporter of militias whom he has compared to Boy Scout groups. He has told reporters that possibly the federal government was responsible for the bombing in Oklahoma City. He is also a popular speaker at Patriot group meetings and is known to have many contacts with the Trochmanns and the Militia of Montana.[9]

In spite of support for militias by various government officials, some state laws have been used to counteract militia violence. In 1982, for instance, SPLC successfully used a Texas law in a suit (*Vietnamese Fisherman's*

Association v. *Knights of the Ku Klux Klan*) to close down a paramilitary camp. "In ruling that the camps were illegal, the court defined military organizations in a way that would distinguish them from Scouts and hunters," SPLC reported. The center also used North Carolina laws to prevent the White Patriot Party from becoming a paramilitary organization.[10]

In April 1996 President Bill Clinton signed Public Law 104-132, sponsored by Senator Robert Dole before he became a candidate for president. Proposed legislation had been under consideration for a year by the House and Senate, and when enacted was titled the Antiterrorism and Effective Death Penalty Act of 1996. It includes numerous provisions for countering international as well as domestic terrorism and authorizes payments to victims of terrorism.

Some observers argue that the Antiterrorism Act was weakened by amendments to the bill before it was signed. One provision, however, attempts to address the kind of terrorist bombing in Oklahoma City linked to men who had ties with armed militias. It "prohibits the possession, or pledge or acceptance as security for a loan, of stolen explosive materials moving in interstate or foreign commerce."

Another section directs the Attorney General to study and report to the Congress concerning:

> (1) the extent to which there is available to the public material that instructs how to make bombs, destructive devices, and weapons of mass destruction and the extent to which information gained from such material has been used in incidents of domestic and international terrorism; (2) the likelihood that

such information may be used in future terrorism incidents; (3) the application of existing Federal laws to such material, any need and utility for additional laws, and an assessment of the extent to which the First Amendment protects such material and its private and commercial distribution.

Free Speech vs. Censorship

Although the First Amendment protects free speech (which includes written and electronically produced materials), some organizations and individuals would like to ban extremist messages. In 1995, for example, Senator Dianne Feinstein of California proposed an amendment to the anti-terrorism bill that would, in her words, make it

> . . . unlawful for any person to teach or demonstrate the making of explosive materials, or to distribute by any means information pertaining to, in whole or in part, the manufacture of explosive materials, if the person intends, or knows that such explosive materials or information will likely be used for, or in furtherance of, an activity that constitutes a Federal criminal offense or a criminal purpose affecting interstate commerce.[11]

Feinstein's amendment passed in the Senate, but it was not introduced in the House and was not part of the act that became law in 1996. Still others have tried to ban extremist messages and information in whatever form such material is presented or distributed. However, Gregory Nojeim, legislative counsel for the American

Civil Liberties Union (ACLU), in testimony before the Senate Judiciary Committee noted:

> The ACLU recognizes that members of some antigovernment groups, particularly those that are heavily-armed and utter fiery or racist rhetoric, strike fear in the hearts of many. While the ACLU does not share these views, we insist that the right to espouse such views be protected. The ACLU has a proud history of defending unpopular speech, and the free speech rights of unpopular groups from across the political spectrum, ranging from the Knights of the Ku Klux Klan to the Communist Party. We believe that if the free speech rights of those characterized as "extremists" can be preserved, the free speech rights of every person are protected.[12]

Vice President Al Gore also opposes censorship and made his views known in a commencement speech at the Massachusetts Institute of Technology by saying:

> . . . a fear of chaos cannot justify unwarranted censorship of free speech, whether that speech occurs in newspapers, on the broadcast airwaves or over the Internet. Our best reaction to the speech we loathe is to speak out, to reject, to respond, even with emotion and fervor. But to censor—no. That has not been our way for 200 years, and it must not become our way now.[13]

Congressional Concerns

There have been congressional hearings on the armed militias, but some members of Congress are convinced that more needs to be done to call attention to these groups. On August 1, 1996, Representative Shelia

Jackson Lee of Texas presented House Concurrent Resolution 206, "Expressing the sense of Congress with respect to the threat to the security of American citizens and the United States Government posed by armed militia and other paramilitary groups and organizations."

Signed by more than forty other congressional members, the Concurrent Resolution begins by pointing out that the federal government and "its agencies are democratic institutions, created by and for the people of the United States . . . [and] derive their purpose and their character from the expressed will of the American people, and may be altered from time to time by peaceful means." Reasons for the resolution were also outlined, including the bombing of the Alfred P. Murrah Federal Building in April 1995 and the Freemen siege in Montana where federal agents "were threatened and held at bay for 81 days in a Montana town while trying to exercise their duty to uphold the law, at a cost of millions of dollars to American taxpayers."

The resolution also points out that "self-described militia and paramilitary organizations and groups have repeatedly denounced the legitimacy of the United States Government." Because these groups promote violence, they are "a grave danger to American citizens and the institutions of American democracy, and threaten the very foundation of freedom and democracy in America." In conclusion, the members of the House of Representatives, with the Senate concurring, resolve that:

> (1) armed conspiracies against the Government of the United States or any of its agencies and personnel should be aggressively identified, dissolved, and their

perpetrators brought to justice by the federal authorities of law enforcement with the greatest dispatch possible;

(2) the illegal possession of firearms, explosives, or any substances or devices of destruction by any individual or group should be prosecuted to the full extent of all applicable laws by the Department of Justice; and

(3) those legally possessing firearms, explosives, or any substance or device of destruction, and involved in any conspiracy to harm or destroy any agency or property of the United States Government, or any official of the United States Government, or any person, should be promptly prosecuted to the full extent of all applicable laws by the Department of Justice, including those designed to protect the United States Government against treason and subversion.[14]

What Is the Way of the Future?

If, as some politicians and watchdog groups believe, Americans should be alert to possible threats from the armed militias, what specifically can individuals do? The SPLC's Militia Task Force has a number of recommendations, such as urging students to participate in local affairs as a way to gain respect for the democratic process. Advice for local clergy is to "join together to expose the perverted ideology that underlies the Identity movement," which is basic to some militia groups. Also the task force suggests balancing the common-law and "patriot" views of the Second Amendment to the United

States Constitution with what the courts have stated about militias and the right to bear arms.[15]

Most of the groups or organizations listed in the back of this book have additional suggestions for actions people can take. The Center for Democratic Renewal (CDR), for example, has published an excellent guide called "When Hate Groups Come to Town." It concentrates on counteracting activities of groups like the KKK and neo-Nazis, but the suggestions apply to armed militias that spread bigoted and hate-filled messages. Among the specifics, CDR stresses the need to document threatening activities with newspaper clippings, reports from harassed victims, and published materials from groups being monitored.

Whatever action is taken to counter armed militias, most Americans do not support the idea that private armies and a civil war are needed to bring about change. Rather, they are likely to say as many activists have, "enough is enough" of warlike talk and threats of violence. Instead of blaming scapegoats, growing numbers of citizens try working with a variety of people to solve real problems. If social, economic, or other policies are unworkable or harmful, true patriots exercise their voting privileges and try to enforce their constitutional rights through the courts. They know, as Congressman Schumer and others have stated, ballots and courts that protect civil rights are better than bullets and bombs.

Where to Find Help

Selected Groups for Information on Armed Militias and Other Extremists:

Alternative Radio
PO Box 551
Boulder, CO 80306

Alternet
Institute for Alternative Journalism
77 Federal Street
San Francisco, CA 94107
(415) 284-1420

American Civil Liberties Union
132 West 43rd Street
New York, NY 10036
(212) 944-9800

American Friends Service Committee
1501 Cherry Street
Philadelphia, PA 19102
(215) 241-7000

American Jewish Committee Institute for Human Relations
165 East 56th Street
New York, NY 10022-2476
(212) 751-4000

American Jewish Congress
15 East 84th Street
New York, NY 10028
(212) 879-4500

Anti-Defamation League of B'nai B'rith
823 United Nations Plaza
New York, NY 10017
(212) 490-2525

Applied Research Center
25 Embarcadero Cove
Oakland, CA 94606
(510) 534-1769

Center for Constitutional Rights
666 Broadway
New York, NY 10012
(212) 614-6464

Center for Democratic Renewal
PO Box 50469
Atlanta, GA 30302
(404) 221-0025

Citizens Project
PO Box 2085
Colorado Springs, CO 80901
(719) 685-9899

**Clearinghouse on
Environmental Advocacy
and Research**
1718 Connecticut Avenue NW,
Suite 600
Washington, DC 20009
(202) 667-6982

**Coalition for Human
Dignity**
PO Box 40344
Portland, OR 97240
(503) 281-5823

**CovertAction Quarterly
CovertAction Publications**
1500 Massachusetts Avenue,
NW Suite 732
Washington, DC 20005
(202) 331-9763

Cult Awareness Network
2421 West Pratt Boulevard,
Suite 1173
Chicago, IL 60645
(312) 267-7777

Data Center
464 19th Street
Oakland, CA 94612
(510) 835-4692

**Facing History and
Ourselves**
16 Hurd Road
Brookline, MA 02146
(617) 232-1595

**Fairness and Accuracy in
Reporting**
130 West 25th Street
New York, NY 10001
(212) 633-6700

**Human Rights Resource
Center**
615 B Street
San Rafael, CA 9490
(415) 453-0404

**Institute for First
Amendment Studies**
PO Box 589
Great Barrington, MA 01230
(413) 528-3800

**Montana Human Rights
Network**
PO Box 9184
Helena, MT 59624
(406) 442-5506

**National Coalition Against
Censorship**
275 7th Avenue, 20th Floor
New York, NY 10001
(212) 807-6222

Northwest Coalition Against Malicious Harassment
PO Box 16776
Seattle, WA 98116
(206) 233-9136

People Against Racist Terror
PO Box 1990
Burbank, CA 91507
(310) 288-5003

People for the American Way
2000 M Street, NW,
Suite 400
Washington, DC 20036
(202) 467-4999

Political Research Associates
120 Beacon Street
Suite 202
Somerville, MA 02143
(617) 661-9313

Poverty & Race Research Action Council
1711 Connecticut Avenue, NW
#217
Washington, DC 20009
(202) 387-9887

Progressive Magazine
409 East Main Street
Madison, WI 53003

Project Tocsin
PO Box 163523
Sacramento, CA 95816-3523
(916) 374-8276

Radio for Peace International
PO Box 20728
Portland, OR 97220
(503) 252-3639

Simon Wiesenthal Center
9760 West Pico
Los Angeles, CA 90035
(310) 553-9036

Southern Poverty Law Center
400 Washington Avenue
Montgomery, AL 36104
(334) 264-0286

Western States Center
522 SW Fifth Avenue,
Suite 1390
Portland, OR 97204
(503) 228-8866

Chapter Notes

Chapter 1

1. Patricia King, "'Vipers' in the 'Burbs,'" *Newsweek,* July 15, 1996, p. 21.

2. William Hermann and Brent Whiting, "Viper Militia Members Hit with 12 New Charges," *Arizona Republic,* October 5, 1996, p. B1.

3. Anti-Defamation League, "Armed & Dangerous: Militias Take Aim at the Federal Government" (an *ADL Fact Finding Report*), 1994. (On the Internet at: http://www.nizkor.org/hweb/orgs/american/adl/)

4. Ibid.

5. John Mintz, "Militias Meet the Senate with Conspiracies to Share," *Washington Post,* June 16, 1995, p. A1.

6. Chip Berlet and Matthew N. Lyons, "Armed Militias and Angry Patriots: Regressive Populism or Neo-Fascism?" (On the Internet, January 15, 1995, pra.reports conference on igc.apc.org)

7. Daniel Junas, "The Rise of Citizen Militias: Angry White Guys with Guns," *CovertAction Quarterly,* Spring 1995, electronic version.

8. David Barsamian, weekly public affairs program, "Alternative Radio," interview with Chip Berlet, May 10, 1995.

9. Paul de Armond, "The Anti-Democratic Movement— More than Militias," June, August 1995. (On the Internet at http://nwcitizen.com/publicgood/reports/nullify.html)

10. Quoted in Anti-Defamation League of B'nai B'rith, "The 'Identity Churches': A Theology of Hate," *ADL Facts,* Spring 1983, p. 7.

11. Joseph Roy, et al., *False Patriots: The Threat of Antigovernment Extremists* (Montgomery, Ala.: Southern Poverty Law Center Klanwatch/Militia Task Force, 1996), p. 31.

12. Jack Anderson, *Inside the NRA: Armed and Dangerous* (Beverly Hills, Calif.: Dove Books, 1996), p. 74.

Chapter 2

1. Sheldon Sheps and Mark Pitcavage, "New Militia FAQ Part One," November 6, 1995. (On the Internet at http://www.sff.net/people/pitman/faq1.htm)

2. John Mahon, *History of the Militia and the National Guard* (New York: Free Press, 1983), p. 36.

3. Sheldon Sheps and Mark Pitcavage, "Militia—History and Law FAQ," September 1995. (On the Internet at http://www.sff.net/people/pitman/faq3.html)

4. Sheps and Pitcavage, November 6, 1995.

5. Quoted in Aaron Epstein, "The Second Amendment, Under the Gun," *Philadelphia Inquirer,* May 21, 1995, p. E3.

6. Jack Anderson, *Inside the NRA: Armed and Dangerous* (Beverly Hills, Calif.: Dove Books, 1996), p. 59.

7. Quoted in Epstein.

8. Kenneth S. Stern, *A Force Upon the Plain: The American Militia Movement and the Politics of Hate* (New York: Simon & Schuster, 1996), p. 113.

9. Philip Jenkins, "Home-Grown Terror," *American Heritage,* September 1995, p. 40.

10. Ibid.

Chapter 3

1. Quoted in James Corcoran, *Bitter Harvest: Gordon Kahl and the Posse Comitatus: Murder in the Heartland* (New York: Viking, 1990), p. 29.

2. Anti-Defamation League of B'nai B'rith, "Paranoia as Patriotism: Far-Right Influences on the Militia Movement," *ADL Special Report,* August 1995, p. 30.

3. Quoted in Corcoran, p. 68.

4. Devin Burghart and Robert Crawford, "Vigilante Justice: Common Law Courts," *CovertAction Quarterly,* Summer 1996, electronic version.

5. Michael Janofsky, "Home-Grown Courts Spring Up as Judicial Arm of Far Right," *The New York Times,* April 17, 1996, electronic version.

6. Associated Press, "Now Operating Under New Name, Posse Comitatus Still Deemed Threat Group," St. Paul Pioneer Press, April 24, 1995, p. 4B. Also Associated Press, "Antigovernment Group Leader Sentenced for Assaulting Officers," St. Paul Pioneer Press, March 31, 1995, p. 3B.

7. Nicholas K. Geranios, "Latest Incidents Linked to Extremists Draw Attention to Northern Idaho," *Seattle Times,* October 20, 1996, p. B1.

8. Pierre Thomas and John Fountain, "W. VA. Militia Men Held in Alleged Plot," *Washington Post,* October 12, 1996, p. A1.

Chapter 4

1. Quoted in "Lawyer Says Feds Out to Get Weaver," *Seattle Times,* September 3, 1992, p. B2.

2. George Lardner, Jr., "Reenactment Indicates Ruby Ridge Probe Has Widened," *Washington Post,* October 26, 1995, p. A4.

3. George Lardner, Jr., "Subcommittee Faults FBI Sniper at Ruby Ridge," *Washington Post,* December 22, 1995, p. A3.

4. Quoted in Dee Norton, "Weaver Backed, 'Feds' Ripped," *Seattle Times,* August 24, 1992.

5. Jack Anderson, *Inside the NRA: Armed and Dangerous* (Beverly Hills, Calif.: Dove Books, 1996), p. 136.

6. "Neo-Nazi's Terrorist Novel: Likely Blueprint for Oklahoma Bombers," *Klanwatch Intelligence Report,* June 1995, p. 4.

7. "Indictment Against McVeigh & Nichols in the United States District Court for the Western District of Oklahoma," Filed August 10, 1995.

8. Ibid.

9. Michael Fortier's confession, filed in the United States District court for the Western District of Oklahoma, August 10, 1995. (On the Internet at http://www.kwtv.com/fortier.jpg)

10. Louis R. Beam, "Leaderless Resistance" (essay), February 1992. (On the Internet at http://www.yosemite.net/beam/ne03001.html)

11. Max Baucus, Testimony before the Senate Judiciary Terrorism, Technology, and Government Information Committee, June 15, 1995.

12. Kathlyn Gay, *Saving the Environment, Debating the Costs* (New York: Franklin Watts, 1996), pp. 21–26.

13. Kenneth Stern, *A Force Upon the Plain: The American Militia Movement and the Politics of Hate* (New York: Simon & Schuster, 1996), p. 123.

Chapter 5

1. Quoted in John Mintz, "NRA Rejects Links to Militias While Vowing to Defeat Clinton," *Washington Post,* May 21, 1995, p. A3.

2. Quoted in Kenneth Stern, *A Force Upon the Plain: The American Militia Movement and the Politics of Hate* (New York: Simon & Schuster, 1996), p. 110.

3. Quoted in Jack Anderson, *Inside the NRA: Armed and Dangerous* (Beverly Hills, Calif.: Dove Books, 1996), pp. 118–119.

4. Quoted in Mintz, p. A3.

5. John E. Yang, "House Votes Repeal of Assault-Gun Ban," *Washington Post*, March 23, 1996, p. A1.

6. Robert Dreyfuss, "Good Morning, Gun Lobby!" *Mother Jones*, July/August 1996, electronic version, no page number. (On the Internet at http://bsd.mojones.com)

7. Marion Hammer, "The High Moral Ground of Freedom," address to the 1996 Annual Meeting of Members of the National Rifle Association of America, April 20, 1996. (On the Internet at http://www.nra.org/backgrounder/am-mh.html)

8. Anderson, p. 12.

9. Jonathan Karl, *The Right to Bear Arms: The Rise of America's New Militias* (New York: HarperPaperbacks, 1995), p. 61.

10. Anderson, pp. 96–97.

11. Anderson, p. 84.

12. Thomas Halpern, David Rosenberg, and Irwin Suall, "Militia Movement: Prescription for Disaster," *USA Today: The Magazine of the American Scene*, January 1996, p. 17.

13. "NRA's Citizen Militia Statement," June 7, 1995. (On the Internet at http://www.shadeslanding.com/firearms/nra.militia.statement.html)

14. "Neal Knox to the 1996 Annual Meeting of Members," April 20, 1996. (On the Internet at http://www.nra.org/backgrounder/am-nk.html)

15. Karl, p. 64.

16. Quoted in Wendy Kaminer, "Second Thoughts on the Second Amendment," *Atlantic Monthly*, March 1996, electronic version.

17. Quoted in Kevin Galvin, Associated Press, "Buchanan Aide Tied to Militias Leaves," *Phoenix Gazette*, February 15, 1996, p. A1.

18. Quoted in Stern, p. 117.

19. Ibid., p. 118.

20. Kenneth Silverstein, "NRA Efforts Draw Local Police Fire," *American City & County,* August 1995, p. 12; Anderson, p. 44.

Chapter 6

1. Quoted in Serge F. Kovaleski and Susan Schmidt, "Bombing's Repercussions Rattle Militias," *Washington Post,* May 6, 1995, p. A1.

2. Anti-Defamation League of B'nai B'rith, "Beyond the Bombing: The Militia Menace Grows," 1995. (On the Internet at http://www.nizkor.org/hweb/orgs/american/adl/beyond-the-bombing/btb-introduction.html)

3. Morris Dees, with James Corcoran, *Gathering Storm: America's Militia Threat* (New York: HarperCollins, 1996), p. 199.

4. *United States of America* v. *Ray Lampley, Cecilia Lampley, Larry Wayne Crow, and John Dare Baird, AKA J.D. Baird,* filed November 10, 1995, in the United States District Court for the Eastern District of Oklahoma.

5. Morris Dees, letter to SPLC members, December 1, 1995.

6. Quoted in Dees, with Corcoran, p. 172.

7. Ibid., p. 21.

8. Kenneth Stern, *A Force Upon the Plain: The American Militia Movement and the Politics of Hate* (New York: Simon & Schuster, 1996), pp. 36–37.

9. Quoted in Serge F. Kovaleski, "'One World' Conspiracies Prompt Montana Militia's Call to Arms," *Washington Post,* April 29, 1995, p. A1.

10. Norman Olson testimony, Hearings on Terrorism, United States Senate, May 25, 1995.

11. Quoted in Stern, p. 102.

12. Mark Pitcavage, "'Patriot' Profile #1: Joe Holland, Calvin Greenup, and the Anti-Tax Militia," March 28, 1996. (On the Internet at http://www.sff.net/people/pitman/holland.html)

13. Ibid.

14. Quoted in Jonathan Karl, *The Right to Bear Arms: The Rise of America's New Militias* (New York: HarperPaperbacks, 1995), p. 34.

15. Ibid., p. 36.

16. Doreen Carvajal, "Onetime Political Satire Becomes a Right-Wing Rage and a Hot Internet Item," *The New York Times,* July 1, 1996, p. D7.

17. Southern California Militia Homepage, no date. (On the Internet at http://la.tcinet.com/~mrjohn/)

18. Southern California Militia Homepage, "Who Are We?" no date. (On the Internet at http://la.tcinet.com/~mrjohn/whoarewe.htm)

19. Lee County Militia/1st. Fla. Regiment/1st. United States Militia, no date. (On the Internet at http://www.tnton-line.com/personal/namrepus)

20. Philip Shenon, "Militias Aim to Lure Elite Army Troops, U.S. Generals Fear," *The New York Times,* March 22, 1996, p. A1.

21. John Flesher, "Militia Groups Hampered by Divided Ranks," *South Bend [Indiana] Tribune,* April 14, 1996, p. B8.

22. Rogers Worthington, "Conspiracy Theories Thrive in Troubled Age," *Chicago Tribune,* May 14, 1995, Section 4, p. 1.

23. Stern, pp. 253–254.

24. Remarks by President Clinton on the Militia Movement, Town Hall Meeting, Billings, Montana, June 1, 1995.

Chapter 7

1. Quoted in Jane Hunter, "Montana Church Workers Keep Eye on Militias," *National Catholic Reporter,* October 20, 1995, p. 13.

2. KCTS-Seattle, "NewsHour Online: Curbing the Militia Movement," Rod Minott reporting, April 24, 1996.

3. Whatcom Human Rights Task Force, "Whatcom Human Rights Task Force Condemns Vigilante Organizing," press release, January 9, 1996.

4. Jonathan Mozzochi, "Militias: Assault on Democracy." (On the Internet at http://www.halcyon.com/burghart/militias.html)

5. Representative Charles E. Schumer, Testimony, Hearing on Violent Antigovernment Groups, November 2, 1995.

6. Ibid.

7. Quoted in Kenneth Stern, *A Force Upon the Plain: The American Militia Movement and the Politics of Hate* (New York: Simon & Schuster, 1996), p. 174.

8. Anti-Defamation League, "Beyond the Bombing: The Militia Menace Grows," *ADL Fact Finding Report,* 1995.

9. Joseph Roy, et al., *False Patriots: The Threat of Antigovernment Extremists* (Montgomery, Ala.: Southern Poverty Law Center Klanwatch/Militia Task Force, 1996), p. 56.

10. Ibid., p. 42.

11. Senator Dianne Feinstein, S Amdt. 1209, June 5, 1995.

12. Gregory T. Nojeim, Testimony before the United States House of Representatives Committee on the Judiciary, Subcommittee on Crime, November 2, 1995.

13. Kevin Gori, "Like Smut, Terrorism Prompts Talk of Internet Censorship," *The New York Times,* June 23, 1996, electronic version.

14. House Concurrent Resolution 206, August 1, 1996.

15. Roy, et al., p. 45.

Further Reading

Books

Anderson, Jack. *Inside the NRA: Armed and Dangerous.* Beverly Hills, Calif.: Dove Books, 1996.

Anti-Defamation League. *Armed and Dangerous: Militias Take Aim at the Federal Government.* New York: Anti-Defamation League, 1994.

Anti-Defamation League. *Beyond the Bombing: The Militia Menace Grows.* New York: Anti-Defamation League, 1995.

Bennett, David H. *The Party of Fear: The American Far Right from Nativism to the Militia Movement.* New York: Vintage Books, 1995.

Berlet, Chip, and Matthew N. Lyons. *Too Close for Comfort: The Fascist Potential of the U.S. Right.* Boston: South End Press, 1995.

Coaltion for Human Dignity. *Against the New World Order: The American Militia Movement.* Portland, Oreg.: Coalition for Human Dignity, 1995.

Coates, James. *Armed and Dangerous: The Rise of the Survivalist Right.* New York: Hill and Wang, 1987.

Corcoran, James. *Bitter Harvest: The Birth of Paramilitary Terrorism in the Heartland.* New York: Viking Penguin, 1995.

106

Crawford, Robert, S. L. Gardner, Jonathan Mozzochi, and R. L. Taylor. *The Northwest Imperative: Documenting a Decade of Hate.* Portland, Oreg.: Coalition for Human Dignity, 1994.

Dees, Morris, with James Corcoran. *Gathering Storm: America's Militia Threat.* New York: HarperCollins, 1996.

George, John. *Nazis, Communists, Klansmen and Others on the Fringe: Political Extremism in America.* Buffalo, NY: Prometheus Books, 1992.

Halpern, Thomas, and Brian Levin. *The Limits of Dissent: The Constitutional Status of Armed Civilian Militias.* Northampton, Mass.: Aletheia Press, 1996.

Hazen, Don, ed. *Militias in America 1995.* San Francisco, Calif.: The Institute for Alternative Journalism, 1995.

Henigan, Dennis A., E. Bruce Nicholson, and David Hemenway. *Guns and the Constitution: The Myth of Second Amendment Protection for Firearms in America.* Northampton, Mass.: Aletheia Press, 1995.

Heymann, Philip B. *Lesson of Waco: Proposed Changes in Federal Law Enforcement.* Washington, D.C.: United States Department of Justice, 1993.

Karl, Jonathan. *The Right to Bear Arms: The Rise of America's New Militias.* New York: HarperPaperbacks, 1995.

LaPierre, Wayne. *Guns, Crime and Freedom.* Washington, D.C.: Regnery Publishing, 1994.

Lewis, James R., ed. *From the Ashes: Making Sense of Waco.* Lanham, Md.: Rowman & Littlefield, 1994.

McCuen, Gary E. *The Militia Movement and Hate Groups in America.* Hudson, Wis.: Gary E. McCuen Publications, 1996.

Ridgeway, James. *Blood in the Face.* New York: Thunder's Mouth Press, 1990.

107

Sargent, Lyman Tower, ed. *Extremism in America.* New York: New York University Press, 1995.

Smith, Brent L. *Terrorism in America: Pipe Bombs and Pipe Dreams.* Albany, N.Y.: State University of New York Press, 1994.

Stern, Kenneth S. *A Force Upon the Plain: The American Militia Movement and the Politics of Hate.* New York: Simon & Schuster, 1996.

Walter, Jess. *Every Knee Shall Bow: The Truth and Tragedy of Ruby Ridge and the Randy Weaver Family.* New York: HarperCollins, 1995.

Periodicals

Barkun, Michael. "Militias, Christian Identity and the Radical Right," *The Christian Century,* August 2, 1995.

Bock, Alan. "Ties That Bind," *National Review,* May 15, 1995.

Corry, John. "Meeting the Enemy," *American Spectator,* July 1995.

Dees, Morris. "Still 'A Recipe for Disaster,'" *USA Weekend,* April 12–14, 1996.

Glastris, Paul. "Patriot Games," *Washington Monthly,* June 1995.

Halpren, Thomas, David Rosenberg, and Irwin Suall. "Militia Movement: Prescription for Disaster," *USA Today: The Magazine of the American Scene,* January 1996.

Hatchett, David. "The Militia Movement: The New Klan?" *Crisis,* August 1995.

Hunter, Jane. "Montana Church Workers Keep Eye on Militias," *National Catholic Reporter,* October 20, 1995.

Jenkins, Philip. "Home-Grown Terror," *American Heritage,* September 1995.

King, Patricia. "'Vipers' in the 'Burbs,'" *Newsweek,* July 15, 1996.

LaPierre, Wayne. "Standing Guard," *American Rifleman,* May 1996.

McIntyre, Thomas. "A Hunter's View: Lines in the Sand," *Sports Afield,* October 1995.

Metaksa, Tanya K. "The Clinton War on Guns," *American Hunter,* June 1996.

Ridgeway, James, and Leonard Zeskind. "Revolution U.S.A.," *Village Voice,* May 2, 1995.

Silverstein, Kenneth. "NRA Efforts Draw Local Police Fire," *American City & County,* August 1995.

Smolowe, Jill. "Enemies of the State: America's 'Patriots' Have a Tough List of Demands," *Time,* May 8, 1995.

Stengel, Richard. "White Right," *New Republic,* May 29, 1995.

Stern, Kenneth S. "Militia Mania: A Growing Danger," *USA Today: The Magazine of the American Scene,* January 1996.

Van Biema, David, et al. "The Message from Mark," *Time,* June 26, 1995.

Walker, Martin. "America's Angry White Males," *World Press Review,* July 1995.

"Wise Use Watch," *National Parks,* July/August 1995.

Zeskind, Leonard. "Armed and Dangerous: The NRA, Militias and White Supremacists Are Fostering a Network of Right Wing Warriors," *Rolling Stone,* November 2, 1995.

Index

110

Patriot Movement, 9, 11, 13
Patriots, 8–10, 28, 34, 41, 51,
     62, 64, 65, 75, 76, 79, 94
People Against Racist Terror
     (PART), 84
Phineas Priests, 33–35
Political Research Associates
     (PRA), 84
Posse Comitatus, 25, 26–32,
     58, 83
prejudice, 14, 79
Presser v. *Illinois*, 6
propaganda, 68, 74, 75, 77, 79,
     88
property rights, 47–48, 50

R
Religious Right, 13
Reno, U.S. Attorney General
     Janet, 55, 87
right-wing groups, 7, 22, 84
Ruby Ridge, Idaho, 36–38, 39,
     54, 68

S
Second Amendment, 22, 23,
     56–57, 75, 93–94
Sixteenth Amendment, 27
Southern Poverty Law Center
     (SPLC), 9, 42, 65, 66, 81,
     88, 89, 93
sovereign citizens, 28–29, 32,
     74

T
terrorism, 9, 38, 47, 52, 69, 89,
     90

*The Protocols of the Learned
     Elders of Zion,* 10–11
The Turner Diaries, 42

U
United Nations, 11, 52, 75
United States Constitution, 9,
     16, 18, 20, 22, 29, 31, 48,
     52
United States Forest Service,
     48–50

V
Vietnam War, 7
violence, 13, 15, 33, 34, 58, 59,
     82, 86, 87, 88, 92, 94
Viper Militia, 5–6

W
Waco, Texas, 39–40, 41, 42, 54,
     73, 88
watchdogs, 40, 81
West Virginia Mountaineer
     Militia, 8, 34
White Patriot Party, 76, 89
white supremacists, 9, 13, 33,
     36, 62, 67, 81
World Trade Center bombing,
     42
World War II, 27, 61
World Wide Web (WWW), 17,
     20, 59, 74–76, 85–86

322.4
GAY

Gay, Kathlyn.

Militias.

$18.95

33035000416310

BAKER & TAYLOR